HiSET®

Practice Questions
Part 1 of 2

DEAR FUTURE EXAM SUCCESS STORY

First of all, **THANK YOU** for purchasing Mometrix study materials!

Second, congratulations! You are one of the few determined test-takers who are committed to doing whatever it takes to excel on your exam. **You have come to the right place.** We developed these practice tests with one goal in mind: to deliver you the best possible approximation of the questions you will see on test day.

Standardized testing is one of the biggest obstacles on your road to success, which only increases the importance of doing well in the high-pressure, high-stakes environment of test day. Your results on this test could have a significant impact on your future, and these practice tests will give you the repetitions you need to build your familiarity and confidence with the test content and format to help you achieve your full potential on test day.

Your success is our success

We would love to hear from you! If you would like to share the story of your exam success or if you have any questions or comments in regard to our products, please contact us at **800-673-8175** or **support@mometrix.com**.

Thanks again for your business and we wish you continued success!

Sincerely,
The Mometrix Test Preparation Team

Table of Contents

Practice Test #1

Language Arts–Reading

Refer to the following for questions 1–3:

Jo's face was a study next day, for the secret rather weighed upon her, and she found it hard not to look mysterious and important. Meg observed it, but did not trouble herself to make inquiries, for she had learned that the best way to manage Jo was by the law of contraries, so she felt sure of being told everything if she did not ask. She was rather surprised, therefore, when the silence remained unbroken, and Jo assumed a patronizing air, which decidedly aggravated Meg, who in turn assumed an air of dignified reserve and devoted herself to her mother. This left Jo to her own devices, for Mrs. March had taken her place as nurse, and bade her rest, exercise, and amuse herself after her long confinement. Amy being gone, Laurie was her only refuge, and much as she enjoyed his society, she rather dreaded him just then, for he was an incorrigible tease, and she feared he would coax the secret from her.

(*Little Women* by Louisa May Alcott)

1. From what point of view is this passage written?

a. First person
b. Second person
c. Third person
d. Fourth person

2. The phrase *was a study* implies that:

a. Jo looked jubilant.
b. Jo looked secretive.
c. Jo looked disheveled.
d. Jo looked angry.

3. What can you infer about Laurie?

a. He was stoic.
b. He was taciturn.
c. He was unruly.
d. He was uncanny.

Refer to the following for questions 4–7:

The Bermuda Triangle

The area known as the Bermuda Triangle has become such a part of popular culture that it can be difficult to separate fact from fiction. The interest first began when five Navy planes vanished in 1945, officially resulting from "causes or reasons unknown." The explanations about other accidents in the Triangle range from the scientific to the supernatural. Researchers have never been able to find anything truly mysterious about what happens in the Bermuda Triangle, if there even is a Bermuda Triangle. What is more, one of the biggest challenges in considering the phenomenon is deciding how much area actually represents the

Bermuda Triangle. Most consider the Triangle to stretch from Miami out to Puerto Rico and to include the island of Bermuda. Others expand the area to include all of the Caribbean islands and to extend eastward as far as the Azores, which are closer to Europe than they are to North America.

The problem with having a larger Bermuda Triangle is that it increases the odds of accidents. There is near-constant travel, by ship and by plane, across the Atlantic, and accidents are expected to occur. In fact, the Bermuda Triangle happens to fall within one of the busiest navigational regions in the world, and the reality of greater activity creates the possibility for more to go wrong. Shipping records suggest that there is not a greater-than-average loss of vessels within the Bermuda Triangle, and many researchers have argued that the reputation of the Triangle makes any accident seem out of the ordinary. In fact, most accidents fall within the expected margin of error. The increase in ships from East Asia no doubt contributes to an increase in accidents. And as for the story of the Navy planes that disappeared within the Triangle, many researchers now conclude that it was the result of mistakes on the part of the pilots who flew into storm clouds, likely became discomposed, and then simply got lost.

4. Which of the following describes this type of writing?

a. Narrative
b. Persuasive
c. Expository
d. Technical

5. Which of the following sentences most accurately summarizes this passage?

a. The problem with having a larger Bermuda Triangle is that it increases the odds of accidents.
b. The area that is called the Bermuda Triangle happens to fall within one of the busiest navigational regions in the world, and the reality of greater activity creates the possibility for more to go wrong.
c. One of the biggest challenges in considering the phenomenon is deciding how much area actually represents the Bermuda Triangle.
d. Researchers have never been able to find anything truly mysterious about what happens in the Bermuda Triangle, if there even is a Bermuda Triangle.

6. With which of the following statements would the author most likely agree?

a. There is no real mystery about the Bermuda Triangle because most events have reasonable explanations.
b. Researchers are wrong to expand the focus of the Triangle to the Azores because this increases the likelihood of accidents.
c. The official statement of "causes or reasons unknown" in the loss of the Navy planes was a deliberate concealment from the Navy.
d. Reducing the legends about the mysteries of the Bermuda Triangle will help to reduce the number of reported accidents or shipping losses in that region.

7. Which of the following should the writer consult for more detailed information about the Bermuda Triangle?

a. An encyclopedia entry about the Bermuda Triangle
b. Travel journal entries from a ship captain who sailed the area frequently
c. A brochure for a resort located in the Bermuda Triangle
d. A biography of someone who disappeared in the Bermuda Triangle

Refer to the following for questions 8–11:

"His pride," said Miss Lucas, "does not offend me so much as pride often does, because there is an excuse for it. One cannot wonder that so very fine a young man, with family, fortune, everything in his favour, should think highly of himself. If I may so express it, he has a right to be proud."

"That is very true," replied Elizabeth, "and I could easily forgive his pride, if he had not mortified mine."

"Pride," observed Mary, who piqued herself upon the solidity of her reflections, "is a very common failing I believe. By all that I have ever read, I am convinced that it is very common indeed, that human nature is particularly prone to it, and that there are very few of us who do not cherish a feeling of self-complacency on the score of some quality or other, real or imaginary. Vanity and pride are different things, though the words are often used synonymously. A person may be proud without being vain. Pride relates more to our opinion of ourselves, vanity to what we would have others think of us."

(*Pride and Prejudice* by Jane Austen)

8. Why doesn't the gentleman's pride offend Miss Lucas?

a. She admires his vanity.
b. It is human nature to be proud.
c. He is poor and homeless.
d. He is handsome and rich.

9. What are Elizabeth's feelings towards the gentleman?

a. She is offended by him.
b. She is proud of him.
c. She wants to get to know him better.
d. She is glad he is rich.

10. Which sentence best states the theme of this passage?

a. Pride and vanity are offensive.
b. Fame and fortune can make a person proud.
c. Every person is proud in one way or another.
d. If you have a fortune, you deserve to be proud.

11. According to the passage, what is the difference between pride and vanity?

a. Pride relates to a person's abilities; vanity relates to a person's looks.
b. Men are proud; women are vain.
c. Pride is what you think of yourself; vanity is what you want others to think of you.
d. Pride is part of human nature; vanity is not.

Refer to the following for questions 12–15:

One of the key features of the music scene in the past decade has been the increasing popularity of outsiders, especially those with a career. In previous decades, amateur status was seen as a lower calling or, at best, a step on the way to professional status, but many musical insiders now believe that amateurs actually constitute an elite group within the music scene, with greater chances of eventual success. Professionals, once able to fully devote themselves to the advancement of their musical careers, now find themselves hamstrung by a variety of factors that were not issues even a decade ago, giving the edge to people who do not depend on music for a livelihood. A number of technological, demographic, and economic factors are to blame for this change.

Full-time musicians always had difficulties making ends meet, but these difficulties have been vastly increased by a changing music scene. The increased popularity of electronic music, mega-bands, and other acts that rely heavily on marketing, theatrics, and expensive effects has made it harder than ever for local acts to draw crowds. The decreasing crowds at coffee houses, bars, and other small venues leave the owners without the ability to pay for live music. Amateurs can still play the same coffee houses as ever, and the lack of a hundred-dollar paycheck at the end of the night is hardly noticed. Professionals, however, have to fight more desperately than ever for those few lucrative gigs.

An even bigger factor has been the rise of digital media in general and digital file sharing in particular. People have been trading copies of music for decades, but in the days of analog tapes there was always a loss. The tape one fan burned for another would be of lesser quality than the original, prompting the recipient to go out and buy the album. Now that music fans can make full-quality copies for little or nothing and distribute them all over the world, it can be very hard for bands to make any money on music sales. Again, this does not make much difference to amateurs, but it robs the professionals of what has traditionally been one of their biggest sources of revenue.

All of this results in a situation so dire for professional musicians that their extra experience often doesn't balance out their lack of economic resources. The amateurs are the only ones who can afford to buy new gear and fix broken equipment, keep their cars in working order to get to shows, and pay to promote their shows. The professionals tend to have to fall back on "day jobs," typically at lower rates and with less opportunity for advancement. Even those professional musicians who are able to supplement their incomes with music lessons, wedding shows, and other traditional jobs are often living at such a low level that they cannot afford to buy the professional equipment they need to keep the higher-paying gigs. A fairly skilled amateur, by contrast, may not have the same level of virtuosity but will be able to fake his way through most of what a professional does at a more competitive rate, which will allow him to play professional shows.

12. The author of this essay is mainly:

a. Arguing for a return to a climate more favorable to professional musicians
b. Examining the causes of the increasing success of amateur musicians over professionals
c. Revealing the psychological toll the current economy takes on professional musicians
d. Disputing the claim that unsuccessful professional musicians simply don't work hard enough

13. Which of the following statements about musicians does the essay most directly support?

a. Bars and coffee houses should be willing to pay a fair wage to professional musicians.
b. The most popular professional bands have not been affected by the changes that plague most professional musicians.
c. It is much easier for amateur musicians to book shows than it was a decade ago.
d. Professional musicians have recently lost some of their most important sources of income.

14. In his discussion of professional musicians in the last paragraph, the author:

a. Indicates that amateurs deserve their new, higher status
b. Shows that in the current climate, professionals may not have the ability to purchase and maintain the tools that they need
c. Points out the decrease in the market for wedding gigs and lessons
d. Predicts a decline in the number of professional musicians

15. According to the essay, amateur musicians are becoming more successful at both amateur and professional gigs because professionals:

a. Exclusively performs high-paying gigs and are unwilling to play in clubs
b. Are not able to relate to ordinary people as well as amateurs can
c. Have financial needs that they are not able to meet in the current musical climate
d. Are in an industry that is particularly susceptible to economic changes

Refer to the following for questions 16–21:

Excerpt of a judicial review summary written by Bernard Schwartz

Judicial review, the power of courts to determine the legality of governmental acts, usually refers to the authority of judges to decide a law's constitutionality. Although state courts exercised judicial review prior to the ratification of the Constitution, the doctrine is most often traced to the landmark US Supreme Court decision *Marbury v. Madison* (1803), which struck down an act of Congress as unconstitutional. In a now classic opinion, Chief Justice John Marshall found the power of judicial review implied in the Constitution's status as "the supreme Law of the Land" prevailing over ordinary laws.

Both federal and state courts have exercised judicial review. Federal courts review federal and state acts to ensure their conformity to the Constitution and the supremacy of federal over state law; state courts review laws to ensure their conformity to the US Constitution and their own state constitutions. The power of judicial review can be exercised by any court in which a constitutional issue arises.

Judicial review gained added importance in the late nineteenth and early twentieth centuries, as courts passed judgement on laws regulating corporate behavior and working conditions. In these years, the Supreme Court repeatedly struck down laws regulating wages, hours of labor, and safety standards. This is often called the Lochner Era, after *Lochner v. New York*, a 1905 decision ruling a New York maximum-hours law unconstitutional on the grounds that it violated the Fourteenth Amendment. During this period, the Supreme Court invalidated no fewer than 228 state laws.

Justice Oliver Wendell Holmes Jr., dissenting from many of these decisions, urged judges to defer to legislatures. In the later 1930s, the Supreme Court adopted the Holmes approach—partly in response to the threat of President Franklin Delano Roosevelt's "court packing" plan of 1937. Deferring to legislative judgement, the Supreme Court thereafter upheld virtually all laws regulating business and property rights, including laws similar to those invalidated during the Lochner Era.

Under the chief justiceship of Earl Warren (1953-1969) and beyond, however, the Court moved toward striking down laws restricting personal rights and liberties guaranteed by the Bill of Rights, particularly measures limiting freedom of expression, freedom of religion, the rights of criminal defendants, equal treatment of the sexes, and the rights of minorities to equal protection of the law. In another extension of judicial review, the Court read new rights into the Constitution, notably the right of privacy (including abortion rights) and invalidated laws restricting those rights. Many other countries, including Germany, Italy, France, and Japan, adopted the principle of judicial review after World War II, making constitutional law one of the more important recent American exports.

16. Which of the following statements about judicial review does the passage best support?

a. States should defer to the federal government when interpreting the Constitution.
b. Judicial review was started due to the Lochner Era.
c. The Constitution overrides state law in some cases.
d. Judicial review was founded by Earl Warren, Chief Justice of the Supreme Court.

17. From the passage, it can be inferred ordinary laws created by lawmakers must be within the framework of the Constitution. Which of the following sentences supports this claim the best?

a. Although state courts exercised...
b. Both federal and state courts...
c. Judicial review gained added importance...
d. During this period, the Supreme...

18. Which of the following words best characterizes the content of the passage?

a. Historical
b. Introspective
c. Prospective
d. Demonstrative

19. The word *ratification* as used in this passage refers to:

a. Endorsement
b. Disapprove
c. Limiting
d. Embargo

20. The word *dissenting* as used in this passage refers to:

a. Headstrong
b. Compatible
c. Obliging
d. Contradictory

21. The explanation of judicial review is based on:

a. Constitutional arguments
b. Chief Justice Warren
c. *Marbury v. Madison*
d. *Lochner v. New York*

Refer to the following for questions 22–33:

Garth

The next morning, she realized that she had slept. This surprised her—so long had sleep been denied to her! She opened her eyes and saw the sun at the window. And then, beside it in the window, the deformed visage of Garth. Quickly, she shut her eyes again, feigning sleep. But he was not fooled. Presently, she heard his voice, soft and kind: "Don't be afraid. I'm your friend. I came to watch you sleep, is all. There now, I am behind the wall. You can open your eyes."

The voice seemed pained and plaintive. The Hungarian opened her eyes and saw the window empty. Steeling herself, she arose, went to it, and looked out. She saw the man below, cowering by the wall, looking grief-stricken and resigned. Making an effort to overcome her revulsion, she spoke to him as kindly as she could.

"Come," she said, but Garth, seeing her lips move, thought she was sending him away. He rose and began to lumber off, his eyes lowered and filled with despair.

"Come!" she cried again, but he continued to move off. Then, she swept from the cell, ran to him, and took his arm. Feeling her touch, Garth trembled uncontrollably. Feeling that she drew him toward her, he lifted his supplicating eye, and his whole face lit up with joy.

She drew him into the garden, where she sat upon a wall, and for a while, they sat and contemplated one another. The more the Hungarian looked at Garth, the more deformities she discovered. The twisted spine, the lone eye, the huge torso over the tiny legs. She couldn't comprehend how a creature so awkwardly constructed could exist. And yet, from the air of sadness and gentleness that pervaded his figure, she began to reconcile herself to it.

"Did you call me back?" asked he.

"Yes," she replied, nodding. He recognized the gesture.

"Ah," he exclaimed. "Do you know that I am deaf?"

"Poor fellow," exclaimed the Hungarian, with an expression of pity.

"You'd think nothing more could be wrong with me," Garth put in, somewhat bitterly, but he was happier than he could ever remember having been.

22. Why was the girl surprised that she had slept?

a. She usually tried to avoid sleeping.
b. It had been a long time since she had had the chance to sleep.
c. She hadn't intended to go to sleep.
d. Garth looked so frightening that she thought he would keep her awake.

23. Why did she shut her eyes again when she saw Garth in the window?

a. She wanted to sleep some more.
b. The sun was so bright that it hurt her eyes.
c. She didn't want to look at Garth.
d. She wanted Garth to think she was still sleeping.

24. What two characteristics are contrasted in Garth?

a. Ugliness and gentleness
b. Fear and merriment
c. Happiness and sadness
d. Anger and fearfulness

25. During this passage, how do the girl's emotions toward Garth change?

a. They go from fear to loathing.
b. They go from anger to fear.
c. They go from fear to disdain.
d. They go from revulsion to pity.

26. Why does the girl have to steel herself to approach the window and look out at Garth?

a. She has not eaten for a long time.
b. She is repelled by his appearance.
c. She is blinded by the sun behind him.
d. The window is open, and it is cold.

27. How does Garth feel toward the girl when he first moves away from the window?

a. He is curious about her.
b. He is sad because she appears to reject him.
c. He is angry at her for pretending to sleep.
d. He expects her to scold him.

28. Why does Garth withdraw from the girl when she first speaks to him?

a. He expects her to hurt him.
b. He misunderstands her because he cannot hear.
c. People are always mean to him.
d. He doesn't want her to feel revulsion because of his appearance.

29. What is a synonym for the word *supplicating*?

a. Castigating
b. Menacing
c. Repeating
d. Begging

30. Why is it surprising that the girl takes Garth's arm?

a. She is engaged to someone else.
b. She has to reach through the window.
c. He is deaf.
d. She was very frightened of him initially.

31. Which of the following adjectives might you use to describe the girl's personality?

a. Determined
b. Robust
c. Contemplative
d. Sympathetic

32. Which of the following adjectives would you use to describe Garth's feelings toward himself?

a. Contemplative
b. Destitute
c. Resentment
d. Deflated

33. Why is Garth so happy in the last sentence?

a. Because he can understand the girl
b. Because he has learned to read lips
c. Because the girl figured out that he is deaf
d. Because the girl seems to accept him

Refer to the following for questions 34–36:

Although technological tools like polygraph tests, psychological theories, and interrogation techniques have resulted in slightly greater accuracy for law enforcement agents catching liars, it is still important to understand the nature of lies and check unfounded assumptions that can lead to unquestioning acceptance of false statements. Because intentional deception is one of the biggest obstacles to a successful criminal investigation, developing the ability to separate dubious or outright false statements from true ones has to be one of the main goals of every police officer and law enforcement investigator. In addition, an officer must be able to quickly sort out the possible repercussions of a false statement and the ways it can affect the rest of an investigation, should one slip by police screening. This is the only way to punish the guilty, exonerate the innocent, and do the most possible good in preventing future crimes.

The most difficult lie to catch is the half-truth. Half-truths are distortions constructed by using a seed of truth as a way to sprout a more convincing lie. A half-truth may incorporate intentional exaggeration or understatement, lies of omission, false implications, or outright lies mixed in with actual facts. Half-truths that slip past the detectives investigating a case are classified as either "smoke" lies or "mirror" lies. Smoke refers to half-truths that slow down an investigation by casting doubt on otherwise promising leads or angles of investigation. Mirrors are lies that manage to send the detective off in the wrong direction altogether, usually by linking a fact to a false supposition.

Most other lies are overt and intentional. Usually, they are told as a way for a suspect or witness to protect himself or his friends or, more rarely, to cast suspicion on a rival. In some cases, these sorts of lies can be compounded by overzealous or corrupt police who want to earn a conviction of a supposed perpetrator at any cost. Particularly in high-profile cases with gruesome details, this sort of lie results in more false convictions than any other type of distortion.

34. Which statement most accurately conveys the essay's main idea?

a. New police techniques have been ineffective at helping investigators catch liars.
b. The worst lies aren't outright lies; they're sneaky half-truths.
c. People in law enforcement need to be able to recognize lies to be effective and just.
d. There are only two primary types of lies.

35. The essay's writer would be most likely to say that a police officer's ability to recognize both lies and half-truths is:

a. Indispensable in a criminal investigation
b. Difficult because of the sophistication of some liars
c. The most important tool that law enforcement has
d. Crucial, but beyond the abilities of most officers

36. According to the essay, "smoke":

a. Is the most frequently told type of half-truth
b. Never contains outright lies mixed in with truth
c. Can slow down an investigation
d. Sends detectives off in the wrong direction altogether

Refer to the following for questions 37–39:

In the United States, where we have more land than people, it is not at all difficult for persons in good health to make money. In this comparatively new field there are so many avenues of success open, so many vocations which are not crowded, that any person of either sex who is willing, at least for the time being, to engage in any respectable occupation that offers, may find lucrative employment.

Those who really desire to attain an independence, have only to set their minds upon it, and adopt the proper means, as they do in regard to any other object which they wish to accomplish, and the thing is easily done. But however easy it may be found to make money, I have no doubt many of my hearers will agree it is the most difficult thing in the world to keep it. The road to wealth is, as Dr. Franklin truly says, "as plain as the road to the mill." It consists simply in expending less than we earn; that seems to be a very simple problem. Mr. Micawber, one of those happy creations of the genial Dickens, puts the case in a strong light when he says that to have annual income of twenty pounds, per annum, and spend twenty pounds and sixpence, is to be the most miserable of men; whereas, to have an income of only twenty pounds, and spend but nineteen pounds and sixpence, is to be the happiest of mortals.

Many of my hearers may say, "we understand this; this is economy, and we know economy is wealth; we know we can't eat our cake and keep it also." Yet I beg to say that perhaps more cases of failure arise from mistakes on this point than almost any other. The fact is, many people think they understand economy when they really do not.

Excerpt from *The Art of Money-Getting* by P.T. Barnum

37. Who is the most likely audience for this passage?

a. Economists
b. General readers
c. Teachers
d. Philanthropists

38. Which word best describes the author's attitude towards those who believe they understand money?

a. Supportive
b. Incriminating
c. Excessive
d. Patronizing

39. This passage is most likely taken from a(n):

a. Self-help manual
b. Autobiography
c. Epistle
d. Novel

Refer to the following for questions 40–42:

Journalists often use a recording device to capture the audio transcript of an interview with a subject. The recording device is thought of as a reliable and efficient way to ensure that all important parts of the interview have been archived, which is something that may be complicated for a journalist to do by hand. Besides being difficult to execute quickly, legibly, and efficiently, taking notes by hand can distract the journalist from the interview subject's body language, verbal cues, or other subtle information that can go unnoticed when the journalist is not fully concentrating on the person talking. These missed cues, for example, noticing that the tough-guy interview subject closed his eyes and trembled slightly when he talked about his recently departed mother, could add an interesting perspective to the article.

However, relying on a recording device is not without troubles. Most journalists can quickly relate stories of disappointments they or co-workers have endured due to problems with equipment. For instance, a journalist may not notice low batteries until it is too late. As a result, a portion of an interview can be lost without any way to reclaim it. The machine's volume can be accidentally left too low to hear the subject on later playback, the recorder may be accidentally switched off during the interview, and any number of other unplanned and unexpected electronic malfunctions can occur to sabotage the recording. While recording device problems may not occur often, even a rate of once a year can be extremely problematic for a writer. Some glitches may be unrealized until hours later when the journalist is prepared to work with the recording.

Most experienced journalists do not rely solely on technology when they are interviewing a subject for an article. Instead, as the recording device creates an audio record of the interview, journalists will simultaneously record their own notes by hand. This dual-note method means that most of the time, a wise journalist has two good resources to use as he or she writes the article draft.

40. According to the passage, which of the following is NOT a reason a recording device can be superior to taking notes by hand?

a. Note taking can be slow.
b. Note taking is unreliable.
c. Note taking forces the writer to look away from the subject.
d. Note taking can be difficult to read later.

41. Which of the following is NOT an example of body language as described by the passage?

a. A quiet answer
b. Shocked look
c. Wringing hands
d. A glance to the side

42. Which statement from the passage best supports the conclusion that taking notes and recording audio during an interview is a good practice for journalists?

a. Journalists often use a recording device to capture the audio transcript of an interview with a subject.
b. Relying on a recording device is not without troubles, however.
c. As a result, a portion of an interview can be lost without any way to reclaim it.
d. This dual-note method means that most of the time, a wise journalist has two good resources to use as he or she writes the article draft.

Refer to the following for questions 43–50:

Passage 1 is adapted from Edmund Burke's Reflections on the Revolution in France, *originally published 1790.*

Passage 2 is adapted from Thomas Paine's Rights of Man, *originally published 1791. Paine's work was written in response to Burke's, regarding the French Revolution.*

Passage 1

When I see the spirit of liberty in action, I see a strong principle at work; and this, for a while, is all I can possibly know of it. The wild gas, the fixed air, is plainly broke loose; but we ought to suspend our judgment until the first effervescence is a little subsided, till the liquor is cleared, and until we see something deeper than the agitation of a troubled and frothy surface. I must be tolerably sure, before I venture publicly to congratulate men upon a blessing, that they have really received one.

Flattery corrupts both the receiver and the giver, and adulation is not of more service to the people than to kings. I should, therefore, suspend my congratulations on the new liberty of France until I was informed how it had been combined with government, with public force, with the discipline and obedience of armies, with the collection of an effective and well-distributed revenue, with morality and religion, with the solidity of property, with peace and order, with civil and social manners. All these (in their way) are good things, too, and without them liberty is not a benefit whilst it lasts, and is not likely to continue long.

The effect of liberty to individuals is that they may do what they please; we ought to see what it will please them to do, before we risk congratulations which may be soon turned into complaints. Prudence would dictate this in the case of separate, insulated, private men, but liberty, when men act in bodies, is power. Considerate people, before they declare themselves, will observe the use which is made of power and particularly of so trying a thing as new power in new persons of whose principles, tempers, and dispositions they have little or no experience, and in situations where those who appear the most stirring in the scene may possibly not be the real movers.

Passage 2

It was not against Louis XVI, but against the despotic principles of the Government, that the nation revolted. These principles had not their origin in him, but in the original establishment, many centuries back: and they were become too deeply rooted to be removed, and the Augean stables of parasites and plunderers too abominably filthy to be cleansed by anything short of a complete and universal Revolution.

When it becomes necessary to do anything, the whole heart and soul should go into the measure, or not attempt it. That crisis was then arrived, and there remained no choice but to act with determined vigor, or not to act at all. The king was known to be the friend of the nation, and this circumstance was favorable to the enterprise. Perhaps no man bred up in the style of an absolute king, ever possessed a heart so little disposed to the exercise of that species of power as the present King of France.

But the principles of the Government itself still remained the same. The Monarch and the Monarchy were distinct and separate things; and it was against the established despotism of the latter, and not against the person or principles of the former, that the revolt commenced, and the Revolution has been carried.

Mr. Burke does not attend to the distinction between men and principles, and, therefore, he does not see that a revolt may take place against the despotism of the latter, while there lies no charge of despotism against the former....

What Mr. Burke considers as a reproach to the French Revolution (that of bringing it forward under a reign more mild than the preceding ones) is one of its highest honors. The Revolutions that have taken place in other European countries, have been excited by personal hatred. The rage was against the man, and he became the victim. But, in the instance of France we see a Revolution generated in the rational contemplation of the Rights of Man, and distinguishing from the beginning between persons and principles. Lay then the axe to the root, and teach governments humanity.

43. In Passage 1, Burke indicates that it is important to:

a. Admire the strong principle of liberty.
b. Wait to rejoice in freedom until it is certain that it will be good for the people.
c. Congratulate those who have received liberty on their blessing.
d. Avoid judging other cultures on their preferred freedoms until they are fully understood.

44. As used in line 7 of Passage 1, *liquor* most nearly means:

a. Strong drink
b. Celebratory champagne
c. Obscuring darkness
d. Haze of excitement

45. What does the author of Passage 1 suggest as a prudent approach to assessing the value of newly acquired liberty in France?

a. Quick support is necessary and effective for maintaining goodwill.
b. The strength of a principle can first be seen by the excitement of the people it affects.
c. Prudence demands suspending congratulations until the situation has been assessed for deeper impacts.
d. New freedoms should be celebrated without regard to their impact on morality, religion, or civil manners.

46. Paine and Burke would most likely agree that:

a. Liberty is the highest gift a person can be given.
b. While the King may love his people, he cannot change centuries of law and tradition.
c. It is important to weigh options carefully before seeking freedom from a government.
d. The original French government was corrupt, and some kind of action was necessary.

47. In the first paragraph of Passage 2, how did Paine justify the French Revolution?

a. The government had been corrupted beyond salvaging, and the only solution was a complete change.
b. The aristocracy was a parasite that was sucking the life out of its people, and the nation would not survive without changing government.
c. Louis XVI's rule was crippling the country, and he needed to be replaced immediately with no chance of reinstatement.
d. The laws were centuries old and were inappropriate for governing the French people.

48. Paine feels that Burke does not understand that:

a. Liberty should be obtained at any cost.
b. Revolting against corrupt principles is not the same as rebelling against the rulers.
c. The King of France actually loved his people.
d. The nation of France was in crisis, and it was necessary to act decisively before it was too late.

49. How would Burke most likely have responded to Paine's statement in lines 44–47 of Passage 2 that the revolution was "generated in the rational contemplation of the Rights of Man"?

a. He would contend that human rights were actually violated by the revolution, not supported.
b. He would point out that human rights cannot be rationally contemplated because they cannot be defined.
c. He would argue that the revolution was not considered rationally, but emotionally.
d. He would state that the people doing the contemplation were not the real movers, and thus their results were invalid.

50. Which of the following choices best represents the relationship between the two passages?

a. Passage 2 provides a different angle to the argument in Passage 1.
b. Passage 2 is a rebuttal to the major claim of Passage 1.
c. Passage 2 gives new evidence that refutes Passage 1.
d. Passage 2 provides supporting evidence for Passage 1.

Language Arts–Writing

Refer to the following for questions 1–5:

(1) Kids and people need to spend more time outside on a daily basis. (2) Last Child in the Woods: Saving Our Children from Nature-Deficit Disorder is by Richard Louv and who says that in the last 30 years kids have become increasingly removed from nature to their detriment. (3) A 1991 study found that the radius children are allowed to roam outside their homes has shrunk to 1/9 of what it was 20 years before.

(4) Very bad for their physical fitness and mental health. (5) One in 5 American children is obese—compared with one in 20 in the late 1960s—and nearly 8 million kids suffer from mental illnesses, including depression and attention deficit disorder. (6) He says playing in nature helps reduce stress, increase concentration and promote problem-solving, this can help kids with attention deficit disorder and many other problems. (7) Nature play can increase a child's self-confidence and independence.

(8) Parents are scared to let kids play in the woods. (9) Parents are increasingly afraid of child abduction. (10) This is a terrible thing but actually very rare and fear of them should be balanced against the effect of fear on our daily lives.

(11) Kids play too many video games, watch too much television and are in the car for long stretches of time. (12) It is important to have the experience of wet feet and dirty hands and not just read about a frog, for example but to hold it in your hands.

(13) Parents and emphasize organized sports over imaginative play. (14) It's great that kids play so much organized sports now, but activity and physical play used to be what kids did with their free time, not twice a week for soccer practice.

1. Consider the following excerpt from the passage.

Sentence 2: *Last Child in the Woods: Saving Our Children from Nature-Deficit Disorder* is by Richard Louv and who says that in the last 30 years kids have become increasingly removed from nature to their detriment.

Select the best version of the underlined portion.

a. is by Richard Louv and who says that in the last 30 years kids have become increasingly removed
b. is by Richard Louv, who says that in the last 30 years kids have become increasingly removed
c. is by Richard Louv and he says that in the last 30 years kids have become increasingly removed
d. is by Richard Louv he says that in the last 30 years kids have become increasingly removed

2. Which of the following is the most succinct and clear way to rewrite sentences 8 and 9?

a. Parents are scared to let kids play in the woods and are increasingly afraid of child abduction.
b. Parents are scared to let kids play in the woods because they are increasingly afraid of child abduction.
c. Parents are scared to let kids play in the woods so they are increasingly afraid of child abduction.
d. Parents are scared to let kids play in the woods or be abducted.

3. Which of the following represents the best version of sentence 4?

a. It is very bad for their physical fitness and mental health.
b. This is very bad for their physical fitness and mental health.
c. Which is very bad for their physical fitness and mental health.
d. This "nature-deficit disorder" is very bad for their physical fitness and mental health.

4. Sentence 10 is poorly written. What can we infer the initial *This* of the sentence refers to?

a. Parents
b. Kids
c. Woods
d. Child abduction

5. The paragraph that includes sentences 11 and 12 does NOT contain a clear point. Which of the following best describes what the author is likely trying to communicate in this paragraph?

a. Nature is important.
b. It is a problem that kids are increasingly entertained by technology rather than by the sensory experience of nature.
c. It is a problem that kids are removed from nature.
d. Kids should get their hands and feet dirty in some way very often.

6. Where should the following sentence be placed in the paragraph below?

Many people have proposed explanations for this drop.

(1) Surveys of criminal activity in the United States have shown that the 1990s marked a significant drop in crimes such as vehicle theft, rape, and murder. (2) Economist Rick Nevin argues that one contributing factor is the ban on lead gasoline in the 70s because lead poisoning in children has been linked with criminal behavior later in life. (3) Other theories include the controversial claim that legalizing abortion has led to fewer unwanted children and, as a result, fewer potential criminals. (4) Some politicians, including Rudy Giuliani, even take personal responsibility, identifying their policies as effective deterrents to crime.

a. After sentence 1
b. After sentence 2
c. After sentence 3
d. After sentence 4

Refer to the following for questions 7–12:

(1) One of the pioneer sculptors of the nineteenth century was Honore Daumier (1810-1879). (2) He is well-known particularly for caricature heads that

were created between 1830 and 1832. (3) His later works anticipate the work of Rodin, what with their highly cut-out surfaces offset by studied, flowing poses.

(4) Although Daumier was one of the first modern sculptors, his work did not serve as an influence to later artists. (5) This is because nearly all of the other artists of the time hardly ever got to see any of it. (6) This is also true of the sculpture of Degas, who was known as a painter rather than a sculptor, and whose sculpture also was not widely exhibited at the time. (7) And yet, Degas was clearly the greatest sculptor of the era. (8) His bronze casts of dancers and horses retain the layered feeling of the wax models that were their first versions. (9) His more complex scenes seem like crosses between sculpture and painting. (10) When looked at more closely, they display a feeling of mass that the painted canvas cannot by itself convey. (11) It is the interplay between the separate masses in these scenes that involves the viewer and gives them their sense of intrigue.

7. Consider the following excerpt from the passage.

Sentence 2: He is well-known particularly for caricature heads that were created between 1830 and 1832.

Select the best version of the underlined portion.

a. NO CHANGE
b. He is well known, particularly
c. He is particularly well known
d. He is well known particularly

8. Consider the following excerpt from the passage.

Sentence 3: His later works anticipate the work of Rodin, what with their highly cut-out surfaces offset by studied, flowing poses.

Select the best version of the underlined portion.

a. NO CHANGE
b. of Rodin; what with highly cut out surfaces
c. of Rodin, with highly cut-out surfaces
d. of Rodin, with cut-out surfaces

9. Which is the best version of sentence 5?

a. NO CHANGE
b. This is because it was almost never exhibited at the time.
c. His work was hardly ever exhibited.
d. This is because they hardly ever saw any of it.

10. What correction should be made to sentence 6?

a. Add "In addition," to the beginning of the sentence.
b. Delete the clause "and whose sculpture was also not widely exhibited at the time."
c. Change the words "sculpture of Degas" to read "work of Degas".
d. Change "This is also true" to "This was also true".

11. Which sentence is best inserted after sentence 7?

a. A large body of his sculpted works can be found in museums today.
b. His paintings were famous even before the time of his death.
c. He made sculptures out of bronze, stone, and even wood.
d. You can see pictures of his work in many books.

12. Which is best added to the beginning of sentence 10?

a. Increasingly,
b. And yet,
c. Beneath this,
d. However,

Refer to the following for questions 13–18:

(1) Passports, internationally, are recognized travel documents that verify their bearers' identity and nationality. (2) A valid US passport is required to enter and leave foreign countries. (3) The only authority to grant issue or verify United States passports is the United States Department of State (DOS). (4) And it does so through the Passport Services Office. (5) This office of the DOS: Bureau of Consular Affairs (CA) provides information and services to American citizens about obtaining, replacing, renewing or correcting/changing a passport.

(6) You are required to apply in person at any of the over 9,000 passport acceptance facilities located throughout the United States to obtain a passport for the first time. (7) You must provide certain supporting documents and two recent photographs of yourself when you apply or renew. (8) Application forms can be completed online using the Passport Application Wizard, but must be printed prior to submission.

(9) The United States issues both traditional passport books and limited use passport card. (10) You may obtain either one or both of these, depending on your travel needs. (11) Additional information for passports, including answers to frequently asked questions, is available through the DOS: National Passport Information Center (NPIC).

13. Which is the best version of sentence 1?

a. NO CHANGE
b. Passports are recognized documents, internationally, that verify their bearers' identity and nationality.
c. Passports are internationally recognized travel documents that verify their bearers' identity and nationality.
d. Internationally, passports are recognized travel documents that verify its bearers' identity and nationality.

14. Consider the following excerpt from the passage.

Sentence 3: <u>The only authority to grant issue or verify United States passports</u> is the United States Department of State (DOS).

Select the best version of the underlined portion.

a. NO CHANGE
b. The only authority to grant, issue or verify United States passports
c. The only authority to grant, issue, or verify United States Passports
d. The only authority to grant, issue, or verify United States passports

15. Consider the following excerpt from the passage.

Sentences 3–4: The only authority to grant issue or verify United States passports <u>is the United States Department of State (DOS). And it does so through the Passport Services Office.</u>

Select the best version of the underlined portion.

a. NO CHANGE
b. is the United States Department of State (DOS): and it does so through the Passport Services Office.
c. is the United States Department of State (DOS); and it does so through the Passport Services Office.
d. is the United States Department of State (DOS), and it does so through the Passport Services Office.

16. Which is the best version of sentence 6?

a. NO CHANGE
b. To obtain a passport for the first time you are required to apply in person at any of the over 9,000 passport acceptance facilities located throughout the United States.
c. To obtain a passport for the first time, you are required to apply in person at any of the over 9,000 passport acceptance facilities located throughout the United States.
d. You are required to apply in person, at any of the over 9,000 passport acceptance facilities located throughout the United States, to obtain a passport for the first time.

17. What is the best version of sentence 9?

a. NO CHANGE
b. The United States issues both traditional passport books and limited use passport cards.
c. The United States issue both traditional passport books and limited use passports card.
d. The United States issues both traditional passport books and limited use's passport card.

18. Which sentence is best inserted after sentence 11?

a. You will probably have to stand in line for a long time.
b. Application forms can be printed online using the Passport Application Wizard.
c. For more information, you can go online at www.travel.state.gov.
d. Remember to get your picture taken for your passport.

19. Where should the following sentence be placed in the paragraph below?

Insects that carry the disease can develop resistance to the chemicals, or insecticides, that are used to kill the mosquitoes.

(1) Malaria, a disease spread by insects and parasites, has long proven to be difficult to treat. (2) Part of the explanation has to do with adaptation, or the ability of one generation to pass its strengths on to another. (3) Some insects are simply not affected by these insecticides. (4) Unfortunately, these are the insects that survive and go on to reproduce, creating another generation of insects that are immune to the current insecticides. (5) Many researchers have abandoned hope for insecticides as a cure for malaria, turning their attention instead to other forms of defense, such as protein-blockers that protect humans from the effects of the disease instead of from the carriers.

a. After sentence 1
b. After sentence 2
c. After sentence 3
d. After sentence 4

Refer to the following for questions 20–25:

(1) The Atlantic hurricane season officially runs from June 1 to November 30. (2) With peak activity occurring August through October. (3) When applied to hurricanes, "Atlantic" generally refers to the entire Atlantic Basin, which included the North Atlantic Ocean, Caribbean Sea and the Gulf of Mexico. (4) To view current tropical weather outlooks and public advisories, please visit the National Hurricane Center's (NHC) website.

(5) For storm information specific to your area in the United States, including possible inland watches and warnings, please monitor your local weather office. (6) For storm information specific to your area outside of the United States, please monitor products issued by your national meteorological service.

(7) In the August 2010 update to the Atlantic hurricane season outlook, the National Oceanic and Atmospheric Administration (NOAA) predicted 14 to 20 named storms, of which eight to 12 could become hurricanes, including four to six major hurricanes of Category 3 strength or higher. (8) The May outlook called for 14 to 23 named storms, including eight to 14 hurricanes and three to seven major hurricanes. (9) Tropical systems acquire a name upon reaching tropical storm strength with sustained winds of at least 39 mph. (10) Tropical storms become hurricanes with winds reach 74 mph, and become major hurricanes when winds reach 111 mph. (11) With six becoming hurricanes, including two major hurricanes, an average season has 11 named storms.

20. Which is the best way to combine sentences 1 and 2?

a. NO CHANGE
b. The Atlantic hurricane season, officially runs from June 1 to November 30 with peak activity occurring August through October.
c. The Atlantic hurricane season officially runs from June 1 to November 30; with peak activity occurring August through October.
d. The Atlantic hurricane season officially runs from June 1 to November 30, with peak activity occurring August through October.

21. Consider the following excerpt from the passage.

Sentence 3: When applied to hurricanes, "Atlantic" generally refers to the entire Atlantic Basin, which included the North Atlantic Ocean, Caribbean Sea and the Gulf of Mexico.

Select the best version of the underlined portion.

a. NO CHANGE
b. which includes the North Atlantic Ocean, Caribbean Sea, and the Gulf of Mexico.
c. which will include the North Atlantic Ocean, Caribbean Sea, and the Gulf of Mexico.
d. which has included the North Atlantic Ocean, Caribbean Sea, and the Gulf of Mexico.

22. Which is the best version of sentence 5?

a. NO CHANGE
b. Including possible inland watches, for storm information specific to your area in the United States, and warnings please monitor your local weather office.
c. For storm information specific to your area in the United States; including possible inland watches and warnings please monitor your local weather office.
d. For storm information specific to your area in the United States including possible inland watches, and warnings please monitor your local weather office.

23. Which of the following would be a good sentence after sentence 9?

a. Typhoons occur in the Pacific Ocean.
b. The naming of tropical storms and hurricanes began in 1953 when the National Weather Service gave the storms female names.
c. NOAA updates its storm predictions regularly.
d. It is best to seek shelter during a hurricane.

24. Consider the following excerpt from the passage.

Sentence 10: <u>Tropical storms become hurricanes with winds reach 74 mph</u> and become major hurricanes when winds reach 111 mph.

Select the best version of the underlined portion.

a. NO CHANGE
b. Tropical storms become hurricanes since winds reach 74 mph
c. Tropical storms become hurricanes when winds reach 74 mph
d. Tropical storms become hurricanes around winds reach 74 mph

25. Which is the best version of sentence 11?

a. NO CHANGE
b. An average season has 11 named storms, with six becoming hurricanes, including two major hurricanes.
c. With six becoming hurricanes including two major hurricanes, an average season has 11 named storms.
d. An average season has 11 named storms, with six becoming hurricanes includes two major hurricanes.

Refer to the following for questions 26–29:

(1) Most scientists agree that while the scientific method is an invaluable methodological tool, it is not a failsafe method for arriving at objective truth. (2) It is debatable, for example, whether a hypothesis can actually be confirmed by evidence.

(3) When the hypothesis is of a form, "All x are y," which is commonly believed that a piece of evidence that is both x and y confirms the hypothesis. (4) For example, for the hypothesis "All monkeys are hairy," a particular monkey that is hairy is thought to be a confirming piece of evidence for the hypothesis. (5) A problem arises when one encounters evidence that disproves a hypothesis: while no scientist would argue that one piece of evidence proves a hypothesis, it is possible for one piece of evidence to disprove a hypothesis. (6) To return to the monkey example, one hairless monkey out of one billion hairy monkeys disproves the hypothesis "All monkeys are hairy." (7) Single pieces of evidence, then, seem to affect a given hypothesis in radically different ways. (8) For this reason, the confirmation of hypotheses is better described as probabilistic.

(9) Hypotheses that can only be proven or disproven based on evidence need to be based on probability because sample sets for such hypotheses are too large. (10) In the monkey example, every single monkey in the history of monkeys would need to be examined before the hypothesis could be proven. (11) By making confirmation a function of probability, one may make provisional or working conclusions that allow for the possibility of a given hypothesis being dissipated in the future. (12) In the monkey case, then, encountering a hairy monkey would slightly raise the probability that "all monkeys are hairy," while encountering a hairless monkey would slightly decrease the probability that "all monkeys are hairy." (13) This method of confirming hypotheses is both counterintuitive and controversial, but it allowed for evidence to equitably effect hypotheses and it does not require infinite sample sets for confirmation or disconfirmation.

26. Consider the following excerpt from the passage.

> Sentences 7–8: Single pieces of evidence, then, seem to affect a given hypothesis in radically <u>different ways. For this reason, the confirmation</u> of hypotheses is better described as probabilistic.

Select the best version of the underlined portion.

a. different ways, but the confirmation
b. different ways; therefore, the confirmation
c. different ways—the confirmation
d. different ways; however, for this reason, the confirmation

27. Consider the following excerpt from the passage.

> Sentence 11: By making confirmation a function of probability, one may make provisional or working conclusions that allow for the possibility of a given hypothesis being <u>dissipated</u> in the future.

Select the best version of the underlined portion.

a. NO CHANGE
b. distilled
c. disconfirmed
d. destroyed

28. Consider the following excerpt from the passage.

> Sentence 13: This method of confirming hypotheses is both counterintuitive and controversial, <u>but it allowed for evidence to equitably effect hypotheses</u> and it does not require infinite sample sets for confirmation or disconfirmation.

Select the best version of the underlined portion.

a. NO CHANGE
b. but it allows for evidence to equitably effect hypotheses,
c. but it allowed for evidence to equitably affect hypotheses,
d. but it allows for evidence to equitably affect hypotheses,

29. This passage ends with, "...it does not require infinite sample sets for confirmation or disconfirmation." This statement refers to information found where in the passage?

a. Most specifically in the initial sentence in this same paragraph
b. Most specifically in the second sentence of the same paragraph
c. Most specifically the fourth sentence of the previous paragraph
d. The information is not found in any paragraph.

Refer to the following for questions 30–31:

(1) The observance of Halloween (All Hallow's Eve) on October 31 has long been associated with images of witches, ghosts, devils and hobgoblins. (2) The holiday dates back to the Celtic festival of Samhain thousands of years ago. (3) The Celts believed that at the time of Samhain the ghosts of the dead were able to mingle with the living. (4) Because that was when the souls of those who had died during the year traveled into the otherworld.

(5) Over the years Halloween customs and rituals have changed. (6) Today, many Americans celebrate the traditions of Halloween by dressing in costumes and telling tales of witches and ghosts. (7) Pumpkins are carved and children go from house to house, knocking on doors and calling out "trick or treat" hoping to have their bags filled with candy. (8) Many communities also celebrate Halloween by holding local parties and parades.

30. Consider the following excerpt from the passage.

Sentence 7: Pumpkins are carved and children go from house to house, <u>knocking on doors and calling out "trick or treat" hoping to have their bags filled with candy.</u>

Select the best version of the underlined portion.

a. NO CHANGE
b. knocking on doors and calling out trick or treat, hoping to have their bags filled with candy.
c. knocking on doors and calling out "trick or treat," hoping to have their bags filled with candy.
d. knocking on doors, and calling out "trick or treat" hoping to have their bags filled with candy.

31. Which would be the best sentence to use before sentence 8?

a. There are lots of adults that enjoy celebrating Halloween just as much as children.
b. There are lots of adults which enjoy celebrating Halloween just as much as children.
c. Just as much as children there are lots of adults who enjoy celebrating Halloween.
d. There are lots of adults who enjoy celebrating Halloween just as much as children.

Refer to the following for questions 32–38:

(1) A new car is second only to a home as the most expensive purchase that many consumers make. (2) According to the National Automobile Dealers Association, the average price of a new car sold in the United States as of February 2010 was $28,400. (3) That's why it's important to know how to make a smart deal.

(4) Think about what car model and options you want and how much you're willing to spend. (5) Do some research. (6) If you do, you'll be less likely to feel pressured

making a hasty or expensive decision at the showroom and more likely to get a better deal.

(7) To get the best possible price by comparing models and prices in ads and at dealer showrooms shop around. (8) You also may want to contact car-buying service and broker-buying service to make comparisons.

(9) Plan to negotiate on price. (10) Dealers may be willing to bargain on their profit margin which is often between 10 and 20 percent. (11) Usually, this is the difference between the manufacturer's suggested retail price (MSRP) and the invoice price.

(12) Because the price is a factor in the dealer's calculations regardless of whether you pay cash or finance your car—and also affects your monthly payments—negotiating the price can save you money.

32. Which is best added to the beginning of sentence 1?

a. However
b. Although
c. Increasingly
d. For example

33. Which is the best version of sentence 2?

a. NO CHANGE
b. The average price, according to the National Automobile Dealers Association, of a new car sold in the United States as of February 2010 was $28,400.
c. According to the National Automobile Dealers Association a new car sold in the United States as of February 2010, was $28,400, the average price.
d. Sold in the United States as of February 2010 was $28,400, accordingly to the National Automobile Dealers Association, the average price of a new car.

34. Consider the following excerpt from the passage.

Sentence 6: If you do, <u>you'll be less likely to feel pressured making a hasty or expensive decision at the showroom</u> and more likely to get a better deal.

Select the best version of the underlined portion.

a. NO CHANGE
b. you'll be less likely to feel pressures making a hasty or expensive decision at the showroom
c. you'll be less likely to feel pressured into making a hasty or expensive decision at the showroom
d. you'll be less likely to feel pressured into making an hasty or expensive decision at the showroom

35. Which is the best version of sentence 7?

a. NO CHANGE
b. By comparing models and prices in ads and at dealer showrooms, shop around, to get the best possible price.
c. To get the best possible price in ads and at dealer showrooms shop around by comparing models and prices.
d. Shop around to get the best possible price by comparing models and prices in ads and at dealer showrooms.

36. Which is the best version of sentence 8?

a. NO CHANGE
b. You also may want to contact car-buying services and broker-buying services to make comparisons.
c. You also may want to contact car-buying services, and broker-buying services, to make comparisons.
d. You'll also may want to contact car-buying services and broker-buying services to make comparisons.

37. Which is the best version of sentence 10?

a. NO CHANGE
b. Dealers may be willing to bargain on their profit margin, which is often between 10 and 20 percent.
c. To bargain on their profit margin dealers may be willing, often between 10 and 20 percent.
d. Often between 10 and 20 percent dealers may be willing to bargain on their profit margin.

38. Consider the following excerpt from the passage.

Sentence 12: Because the price is a factor in the dealer's calculations regardless of whether you pay cash or finance your car—and also affects your monthly payments—negotiating the price can save you money.

Select the best version of the underlined portion.

a. NO CHANGE
b. Because the price is a factor in the dealer's calculations regardless of whether you pay cash or finance your car, and also affects your monthly payments,
c. Because the price is a factor in the dealer's calculations, regardless of whether you pay cash or finance your car (it also affects your monthly payments),
d. Because the price is a factor in the dealer's calculations, regardless of whether you pay cash or finance your car, and also affects your monthly payments—

39. Which sentence does NOT belong in the following paragraph?

(1) Though Thomas Jefferson's taste for expensive home furnishings and wine contributed to the substantial debts he faced toward the end of his life, many other factors also contributed. (2) For instance, when Jefferson's father-in-law died, all of his debts were transferred to Jefferson. (3) Additionally, though his holdings in land and slaves were considerable, they were never especially profitable. (4) Jefferson is believed to have fathered children with one of his slaves. (5) Finally, less than a decade before his death, Jefferson unwisely agreed to endorse a $20,000 loan for a friend, and when the friend unexpectedly died a year later, Jefferson inherited yet another large debt. (6) Jefferson's personal experience with debt may have been part of his motivation in criticizing policies that would increase the national debt.

a. Sentence 2
b. Sentence 3
c. Sentence 4
d. Sentence 5

Refer to the following for questions 40–45:

(1) New rules limit the fees that banks and other financial institutions can charge on some services, so it's possibly that the costs of other services could go up. (2) In the spring 2010 issue of FDIC Consumer News, we discussed how to avoid potential

interest rate and fee increases for credit cards. (3) And here, from expectations that banks will be adding new fees or requirements on bank accounts—such as by discontinuing or limiting free checking services—we focus on ways that careful consumers can avoid unnecessary costs on their deposit accounts.

(4) Comparison shop so you don't pay more for accounts than you have to. (5) Look at what is being offered by your bank and a few competitors. (6) If your bank is among those that eliminates its free checking services, you may still be able to find another bank offering them, especially if you sign up for direct deposit or electronic statements, or if you conduct a certain number of transactions each month.

(7) In today's low-interest rate environment, it must be better to choose a free account that pays no interest or only a small amount of interest instead of selecting an account that pays a modest interest rate but imposes a monthly fee. (8) Similarly, it may be better to maintain a balance and avoid a monthly fee rather than putting that money in an account and paying a modest interest rate. (9) In both cases, any interest you would earn will probably be a lot less than the monthly fee, which can be $10 or higher.

40. Consider the following excerpt from the passage.

Sentence 1: New rules limit the fees that banks and other financial institutions can charge on some services, <u>so it's possibly that the costs of other services could go up</u>.

Select the best version of the underlined portion.

a. NO CHANGE
b. so it's possible that the costs of other services could go up.
c. so it's possible that the costs of other services can go up.
d. so it's possibility that the costs of other services could go up.

41. Consider the following excerpt from the passage.

Sentence 3: <u>And here, from expectations that banks will be adding new fees or requirements on bank accounts</u>—such as by discontinuing or limiting free checking services—we focus on ways that careful consumers can avoid unnecessary costs on their deposit accounts.

Select the best version of the underlined portion.

a. NO CHANGE
b. And here, from expectations that banks will be adding new fees or requirements within bank accounts
c. And here, with expectations that banks will be adding new fees or requirements on bank accounts
d. And then, with expectations that banks will be adding new fees or requirements on bank accounts

42. Which is the best version of sentence 4?

a. NO CHANGE
b. Comparison shop so you don't paying more for accounts than you have to.
c. Comparison shop so you don't pays more for accounts than you have to.
d. Comparison shop so you didn't pay more for accounts than you have to.

43. Consider the following excerpt from the passage.

Sentence 6: If your bank is among those that eliminates its free checking services, you may still be able to find another bank offering them, especially if you sign up for direct deposit or electronic statements, or if you conduct a certain number of transactions each month.

Select the best version of the underlined portion.

a. NO CHANGE
b. If your bank is among those that eliminates their free checking services;
c. If your bank is within those that eliminates its free checking services,
d. If your bank is among those that eliminate their free checking services,

44. Consider the following excerpt from the passage.

Sentence 7: In today's low-interest rate environment, it must be better to choose a free account that pays no interest or only a small amount of interest instead of selecting an account that pays a modest interest rate but imposes a monthly fee.

Select the best version of the underlined portion.

a. NO CHANGE
b. In today's low-interest rate environment, it might be better to choose a free account that pays no interest
c. It might be better to choose a free account that pays no interest, in today's low-interest rate environment,
d. In today's low-interest rate environment, it might be better to have chosen a free account that pays no interest

45. Which is the best version of sentence 9?

a. NO CHANGE
b. Any interest you would earn is probably a lot less than the monthly fee, which can be $10 or higher, in both cases.
c. In both cases, any interest you would earn will probably be a lot less then the monthly fee, which can be $10 or higher.
d. In any cases, any interest you would earn will probably be a lot less than the monthly fee, which could be $10 or higher.

Refer to the following for questions 46–49:

(1) The United States Department of Agriculture Forest Service has reached a milestone. (2) It now protects more than two million acres of private forests threatened by development. (3) The Forest Service's Northeastern Area helped the agency reach the milestone when the state of Ohio purchased a 15,494-acre property as the new Vinton Furnace State Experimental Forest approximately 90 miles south of Columbus. (4) The milestone was achieved through public-private partnership using federal and leveraged funds of approximately $1.1 billion through the Forest legacy program. (5) The Legacy program has leveraged the federal investment of more than 50 percent of project costs. (6) To date, through non-federal matching funds, to these efforts, more than $630 million has been contributed.

(7) The Forest Legacy program works with private landowners, states and conservation groups to promote sustainable, working forests. (8) Roughly 57

percent of the nation's forests are privately owned, yet the country has lost 15 million acres of private working forests in the last 10 years, with an additional 22 million acres projected to be at risk in the next decade. (9) The Forest Legacy has protected millions of acres of privately owned forests that could have been turned into strip malls and housing developments, say Forest Service experts. (10) They say there have been many success stories, which they are proud of.

46. Which is the best version of sentence 2?

a. NO CHANGE
b. It now protect more than two million acres of private forests threatened by development.
c. It now has protected more than two million acres of private forests threatened by development.
d. It now has been protecting more than two million acres of private forests threatened by development.

47. Consider the following excerpt from the passage.

Sentence 3: The Forest Service's Northeastern Area helped the agency reach the milestone when the state of Ohio purchased a 15,494-acre property as the new Vinton Furnace State Experimental Forest approximately 90 miles south of Columbus.

Select the best version of the underlined portion.

a. NO CHANGE
b. The Forest Services Northeastern Area helped the agency reaching the milestone
c. The Forests' Services Northeastern Area helped the agency reach the milestone
d. The Forest Services Northeastern Area helped the agency reach a milestones

48. Consider the following excerpt from the passage.

Sentence 4: The milestone was achieved through public-private partnership using federal and leveraged funds of approximately $1.1 billion through the Forest legacy program.

Select the best version of the underlined portion.

a. NO CHANGE
b. using federal and leveraged funds of approximately $1.1 billion through the forest legacy program.
c. using federal and leveraged funds of approximately $1.1 billion through The Forest legacy program.
d. using federal and leveraged funds of approximately $1.1 billion through the Forest Legacy program.

49. Which is the best version of sentence 6?

a. NO CHANGE
b. To date, more than $630 million has been contributed to these efforts through non-federal matching funds.
c. Through non-federal matching funds, to these efforts, more than $630 million, to date, has been contributed.
d. To these efforts, through non-federal matching funds, more than $630 million has been contributed, to date.

50. Which sentence does NOT belong in the following paragraph?

(1) Renowned scientist Richard Feynman once said that the atomic theory is one of the most profound discoveries scientists have made. (2) Feynman was also an accomplished percussionist who could play nine beats with one hand while playing ten with the other! (3) "All things are made of atoms," explained Feynman, "little particles that...move around in perpetual motion, attracting each other when they are a little distance apart, but repelling upon being squeezed into one another." (4) He then made the claim that this idea is one of the most illuminating ideas in the history of science: "In that one sentence, you will see, there is an enormous amount of information about the world, if just a little imagination and thinking are applied."

a. Sentence 1
b. Sentence 2
c. Sentence 3
d. Sentence 4

Refer to the following for questions 51–60:

The History of the Calendar

A

(1) Throughout human history, mankind sought to track the days and seasons. (2) Tracing back millennia, archaeologists have discovered calendars, showing the ancient views of the Earth's movement and time's passage. (3) Though most calendars are very similar in length, a few changes have been made as measurements have become more precise.

B

(4) Some calendars have been used for much of recorded human history. (5) For instance; the Assyrian calendar has been in use for over 6,750 years. (6) Many communities still celebrate the Assyrian New Year every spring.

C

(7) The earliest known calendar was discovered in Scotland—twelve pits with a corresponding arc. (8) Researchers have categorized it as a lunar calendar, the phases of the moon are the basis for this.

D

(9) Although Scotland is home to the oldest calendar, most current ones are termed solar calendars. (10) That is, they are based on the fact that the Earth travels around the Sun in a certain number of days. (11) However, several cultures created lunisolar calendars, using both solar and lunar measurements to determine the year and months. (12) The Chinese calendar (that is no longer the country's official calendar but is still used in many places) was originally a lunisolar calendar, with the length of the year based on the sun, however the new year beginning on the new moon before the winter solstice. (13) Lunisolar calendars use intercalary months (a technique similar to a leap day) to add sufficient days to make the lunar months add up to the solar year. (14) Some years have 12 months, but every second or third year, an intercalary month is added to keep the months aligned with the seasons.

E

(15) In 46 BC, Julius Caesar instituted the Julian calendar, a solar calendar that becomes the predominant method of measurement in the Western world for over 1600 years. (16) Before this, the Roman calendar was often stabilized by political goals: years were lengthened or shortened to adjust terms of office (since many offices were held for a year), depending on who was in power. (17) To fix this political issue, Caesar consulted with an Egyptian astronomer, who advised him to adopt a solar calendar. (18) This calendar brought stability, but after Caesar's assassination, the Roman priests mistakenly added too many leap days.

F

(19) Because of this, Easter moved farther from the vernal equinox, so in 1582 AD Pope Gregory XIII introduced a revised calendar, shifted the date forward ten days. (20) Rather than adding an intercalary month every few years, this Gregorian calendar adds a leap day every four years (with a few exceptions), measuring the solar year as 365.2425 days. (21) Though still imprecise, this number is widely accepted worldwide and allows mankind to do what he has attempted throughout history: to keep the year in sync with the seasons.

51. Consider the following excerpt from the passage.

Sentence 1: Throughout human history, mankind <u>sought</u> to track the days and seasons.

Select the best version of the underlined portion.

a. NO CHANGE
b. seeks
c. has sought
d. is seeking

52. Consider the following excerpt from the passage.

Sentence 2: <u>Tracing back millennia, archaeologists have discovered calendars,</u> showing the ancient views of the Earth's movement and time's passage.

Select the best version of the underlined portion.

a. NO CHANGE
b. Tracing back millennia, calendars were discovered,
c. Calendars tracing back millennia have been discovered by archaeologists
d. Archaeologists have discovered calendars tracing back millennia,

53. Consider the following excerpt from the passage.

Sentence 8: Researchers have categorized it as a lunar calendar, <u>the phases of the moon are the basis for this</u>.

Select the best version of the underlined portion.

a. NO CHANGE
b. based on the phases of the moon
c. using the phases of the moon as its basis
d. with its basis being the phases of the moon

54. Consider the following excerpt from the passage.

Sentence 9: Although Scotland is home to the oldest calendar, most current ones are termed solar calendars.

Select the best version of the underlined portion.

a. NO CHANGE
b. Because the Earth travels around the Sun
c. While many of the oldest calendars were lunar
d. Despite the phases of the moon used for many calendars

55. Consider the following excerpt from the passage.

Sentence 11: However, several cultures created lunisolar calendars, using both solar and lunar measurements to determine the year and months.

Select the best version of the underlined portion.

a. NO CHANGE
b. either solar or lunar
c. neither solar nor lunar
d. solar and/or lunar

56. Consider the following excerpt from the passage.

Sentence 12: The Chinese calendar (that is no longer the country's official calendar but is still used in many places) was originally a lunisolar calendar, with the length of the year based on the sun, however the new year beginning on the new moon before the winter solstice.

Select the best version of the underlined portion.

a. NO CHANGE
b. which
c. how
d. what

57. Consider the following excerpt from the passage:

Sentence 12: The Chinese calendar (that is no longer the country's official calendar but is still used in many places) was originally a lunisolar calendar, with the length of the year based on the sun, however the new year beginning on the new moon before the winter solstice.

Select the best version of the underlined portion.

a. NO CHANGE
b. Sun; however
c. Sun, although
d. Sun and

58. Consider the following excerpt from the passage.

Sentence 16: Before this, the Roman calendar was often stabilized by political goals: years were lengthened or shortened to adjust terms of office (since many offices were held for a year), depending on who was in power.

Select the best version of the underlined portion.

a. NO CHANGE
b. renamed
c. skewed
d. torn

59. Should sentence 17 be left in, moved within, or removed from paragraph E?

a. It should be left where it is as a response to the calendar's adjustment to further political goals.
b. It should be moved to the end of the paragraph as a response to the mistake of too many leap days.
c. It should be removed from the paragraph because solar calendars have already been discussed in a previous paragraph.
d. It should be removed from the paragraph because it does not add relevant information.

60. Consider the following excerpt from the passage.

Sentence 19: Because of this, Easter moved farther from the vernal equinox, so in 1582 AD Pope Gregory XIII introduced a revised calendar, shifted the date forward ten days.

Select the best version of the underlined portion.

a. NO CHANGE
b. therefore he shifted
c. he shifted
d. shifting

Essay Question

1. Merit pay for teachers is the practice of giving increased pay based upon the improvement in student performance. It is a controversial idea among educators and policy makers. Those who support this idea say that, with it, school districts are able to select and retain the best teachers and to improve student performance. Others argue that merit pay systems lead to teacher competition for the best students and to test-driven teaching practices that are detrimental to the overall quality of education.

***In your essay, select either of these points of view, or suggest an alternative approach, and make a case for it. Use specific reasons and appropriate examples* to support your position and to show how it is superior to the others.**

Mathematics

1. If $10x + 2 = 7$, what is the value of $2x$?

a. -0.5
b. 0.5
c. 1
d. 5

2. A long-distance runner does a first lap around a track in exactly 50 seconds. As she tires, each subsequent lap takes 20% longer than the previous one. How long does she take to run 3 laps?

a. 172 seconds
b. 160 seconds
c. 180 seconds
d. 182 seconds

3. A woman wants to park her 15-foot-long car in a garage that is 19 feet long. How far from the front of the garage will the front of her car need to be so that the car is centered on the floor of the garage?

a. 2 feet
b. $2\frac{1}{2}$ feet
c. 3 feet
d. $3\frac{1}{2}$ feet

4. Solve the system of equations.

$$3x + 4y = 2$$
$$2x + 6y = -2$$

a. $\left(0, \frac{1}{2}\right)$
b. $\left(\frac{2}{5}, \frac{1}{5}\right)$
c. $(2, -1)$
d. $\left(-1, \frac{5}{4}\right)$

5. John buys 100 shares of stock at \$100 per share. The price goes up by 10%, and he sells 50 shares. Then, prices drop by 10%, and he sells his remaining 50 shares. How much did he get for the last 50 shares?

a. \$4,900
b. \$4,950
c. \$5,000
d. \$5,500

6. The sides of a triangle are equal to integer values of units. Two sides are 4 and 6 units long, respectively. What is the minimum value for the triangle's perimeter?

a. 10 units
b. 11 units
c. 12 units
d. 13 units

7. Herbert plans to use the earnings from his lemonade stand, according to the table below, for the first month of operations. If he buys $70 worth of lemons, how much profit does he take home?

Cash Flow Item	Percentage of Total Earning Used on Item
Lemons	35%
Sugar	20%
Cups	25%
Stand improvements	5%
Profits	15%

a. $15
b. $20
c. $30
d. $35

8. A teacher has 3 hours to grade all the papers submitted by the 35 students in her class. She gets through the first 5 papers in 30 minutes. How much faster does she have to work to grade the remaining papers in the allotted time?

a. 10%
b. 15%
c. 20%
d. 25%

9. A sailor judges the distance to a lighthouse by holding a ruler at arm's length and measuring the apparent height of the lighthouse. He knows that the lighthouse is actually 60 feet tall. If it appears to be 3 inches tall when the ruler is held 2 feet from his eye, how far away is it?

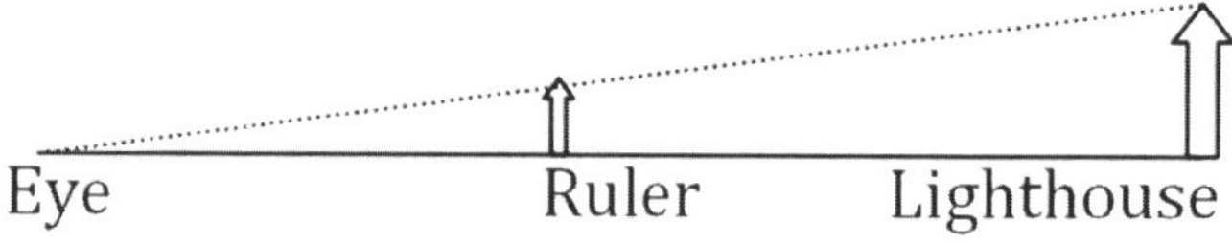

a. 60 feet
b. 120 feet
c. 240 feet
d. 480 feet

10. If $x^2 - 4 = 45$, then which of the following is a value of x?

a. 9
b. 5
c. 3
d. -7

11. What is the value of the product of the first two prime numbers that are larger than 10 divided by the largest prime number smaller than 30?

a. 4.93
b. 3.67
c. 3.18
d. 3.79

12. Determine the volume of a rectangular box with a length of 5 inches, a height of 7 inches, and a width of 9 inches. Round to the nearest inch.

a. 445 in^3
b. 315 in^3
c. 45 in^3
d. 35 in^3

13. What is the greatest integer value of y for which $5y - 20 < 0$?

a. 5
b. 4
c. 3
d. 2

14. A commuter survey counts the people riding in cars on a highway in the morning. Each car contains only one man, only one woman, or both one man and one woman. Out of 25 cars, 13 contain a woman and 20 contain a man. How many contain both a man and a woman?

a. 0
b. 7
c. 8
d. 12

15. Which equation is represented by the graph shown below?

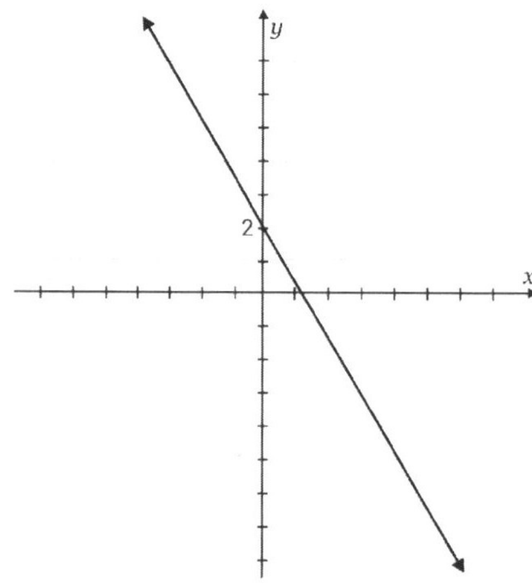

a. $y = \frac{5}{3}x + 2$
b. $y = -\frac{5}{3}x - 2$
c. $y = -\frac{5}{3}x + 2$
d. $y = \frac{5}{3}x - 2$

16. If x is a negative integer and $5 < |x - 3| < 7$, what is the value of $|x|$?

a. -3
b. 0
c. 3
d. 9

17. The right circular cylinder shown in the figure below has a height of 10 units and a radius of 1 unit. Points O and P are the centers of the top and bottom surfaces, respectively. A slice is cut from the cylinder as shown, so that the angle at the top, O, is 60 degrees, and the angle at the bottom, P, is 60 degrees. What is the volume of the slice?

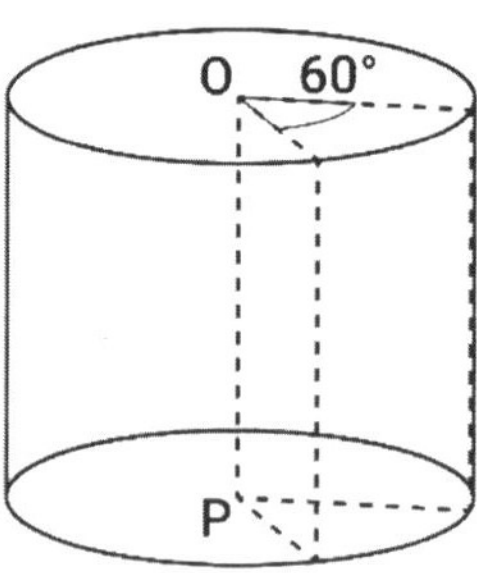

a. 31.4 units^3
b. 5.23 units^3
c. 10.47 units^3
d. 7.85 units^3

18. Which of these functions includes 2 as an element of the domain and -3 as an element of the range?

a. $y = \frac{1}{x+1} - 3$
b. $y = \sqrt{x-2} - 3$
c. $y = |x-1| + 3$
d. $y = \begin{cases} -2x & x < -1 \\ x+3 & x \geq -1 \end{cases}$

19. If Q is divisible by 2 and 7, which of the following is also divisible by 2 and 7?

a. $Q + 2$
b. $Q + 7$
c. $Q + 28$
d. $Q + 9$

20. There are 400 fish in a tank. 150 are blue, 150 are red, and the remainder are brown. Tranh dips a net into the tank and pulls out one fish. The probability of pulling out any single fish is the same. What is the probability, as a percentage, that the fish he pulls out is brown?

a. 50.0%
b. 37.5%
c. 33.3%
d. 25.0%

21. If $a = 3$ and $b = -2$, what is the value of $a^2 + 3ab - b^2$?

a. -13
b. -4
c. 5
d. 12

22. Jack and Kevin play in a basketball game. If the ratio of points scored by Jack to points scored by Kevin is 4 to 3, which of the following could NOT be the total number of points scored by the two boys?

a. 7
b. 14
c. 16
d. 28

23. Factor the following expression: $x^2 + x - 12$

a. $(x-2)(x+6)$
b. $(x+6)(x-2)$
c. $(x-4)(x+3)$
d. $(x+4)(x-3)$

24. Five less than three times a number is equal to 58. What is the number?

a. $-17\frac{2}{3}$
b. $17\frac{2}{3}$
c. 21
d. 169

25. The average of six numbers is 4. If the average of two of those numbers is 2, what is the average of the other four numbers?

a. 5
b. 6
c. 7
d. 8

26. What is the intersection of two lines formed by the equations $y = 2x + 3$ and $y = x - 5$?

a. (5,3)
b. (8,13)
c. (−4,13)
d. (−8,−13)

27. A function $f(x)$ is defined by $f(x) = 2x^2 + 7$. What is the value of $2f(x) - 3$?

a. $4x^2 + 11$
b. $4x^4 + 11$
c. $x^2 + 11$
d. $4x^2 + 14$

28. How many 3-inch segments can a 4.5-yard line be divided into?

a. 15
b. 45
c. 54
d. 64

29. A dress is marked down by 20% and placed on a clearance rack, under a sign reading "Take an extra 25% off already reduced merchandise." What fraction of the original price is the final sale price of the dress?

a. $\frac{2}{5}$
b. $\frac{9}{20}$
c. $\frac{3}{5}$
d. $\frac{11}{20}$

30. The formula for finding the volume of a cone is $V = \frac{1}{3}\pi r^2 h$. Which of the following equations is correctly solved for r?

a. $r = \frac{1}{3}\pi h$
b. $r = \sqrt{\frac{3V}{\pi h}}$
c. $r = \frac{3V}{\pi h}$
d. $r = V - \frac{1}{3}\pi h$

31. Forty students in a class take a test that is graded on a scale of 1 to 10. The histogram in the figure shows the grade distribution, with the x-axis representing the grades and the y-axis representing the number of students who obtained each grade. If the mean, median, and mode values are represented by n, p, and q, respectively, which of the following is true?

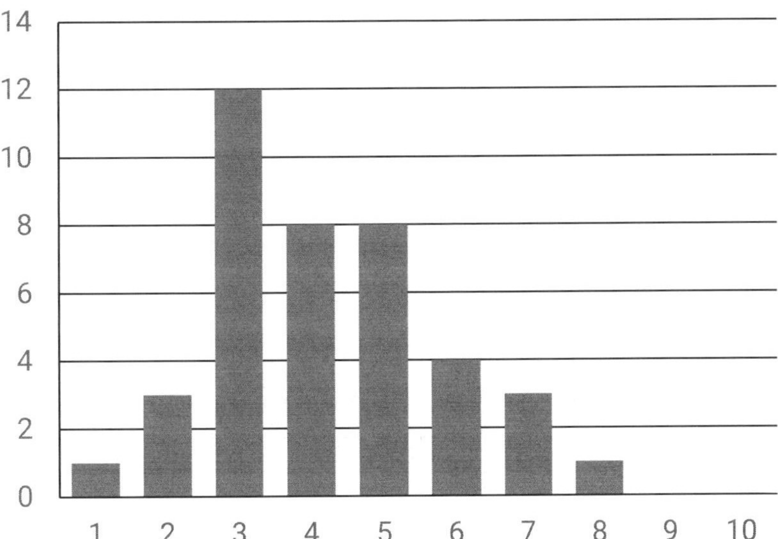

a. $n > p > q$
b. $n > q > p$
c. $q > p > n$
d. $p > q > n$

32. If x and y are positive integers, which of the following expressions is equivalent to $(xy)^{7y} - (xy)^y$?

a. $(xy)^{6y}$
b. $(xy)^{7y-1}$
c. $(xy)^y[(xy)^7 - 1]$
d. $(xy)^y[(xy)^{6y} - 1]$

33. The average of three numbers x, y, and z is 23. The average of three numbers a, b, and c is also 23. What is the average of all six numbers a, b, c, x, y, and z?

a. 11.5
b. 23
c. 34.5
d. 46

34. In the system of equations below, what is the value of $2x + y$?

$$\begin{cases} 2x + y + 7a = 50 \\ 2x + y + 5a = 40 \end{cases}$$

35. If $(6a)x^2 = 30$, then ax^2 is:

a. 6
b. 5
c. 30
d. $\frac{\sqrt{30}}{6}$

36. In a game played with toothpicks, players A and B take turns removing toothpicks from a row on a table. At each turn, each player must remove 1, 2, or 3 toothpicks from the row. The object is to force the other player to remove the last toothpick. If there are 6 toothpicks in the row, which of the following moves ensures a win?

a. Remove 1
b. Remove 2
c. Remove 3
d. Remove 1 or 2

37. A student begins solving the linear inequality $3x - 7 < 20$ as follows.

$$3x - 7 < 20$$
$$x - 7 < \frac{20}{3}$$

When asked to justify this first step, the student replies, "I divided both sides by 3." How would you evaluate this step and the student's justification?

a. Dividing both sides of the inequality by 3 is an uncommon, yet correct, first step, but the student carried it out incorrectly by failing to apply the distributive property on the left side of the inequality.
b. Dividing both sides of the inequality by 3 is a correct first step, and the student carried it out correctly.
c. Dividing both sides of the inequality by 3 is an incorrect first step. The correct first step is to subtract 7 to both sides of the inequality.
d. Dividing both sides of the inequality by 3 is an incorrect first step. The correct first step is to subtract 7 to both sides of the inequality and reverse the direction of the inequality.

38. A water sprinkler covers a circular area with a radius of 6 feet. If the water pressure is increased so that the radius increases to 8 feet, by approximately how much is the area covered by the water increased? Use 3.14 for π.

a. 4 square feet
b. 36 square feet
c. 64 square feet
d. 88 square feet

39. The graph below, not drawn to scale, shows a straight line passing through the origin. Point P_1 has the (x, y) coordinates (-5, -3). What is the x-coordinate of point P_2 if its y-coordinate is 3?

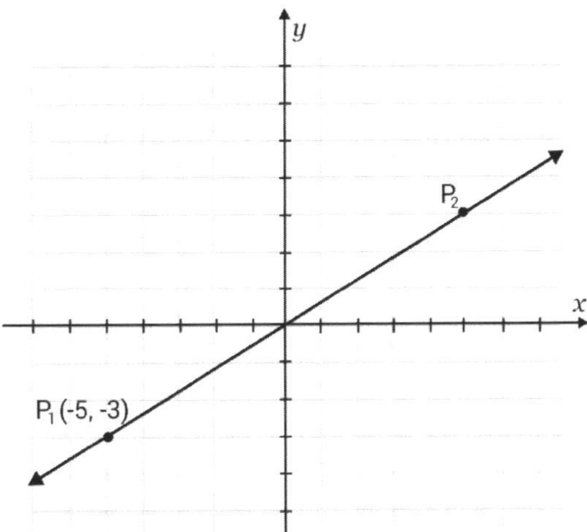

a. 0.8
b. 1
c. 5
d. 3

40. What is the area of an isosceles triangle inscribed in a circle of radius r if the base of the triangle is the diameter of the circle?

a. r^2
b. $2r^2$
c. πr^2
d. $2\pi r$

41. A regular deck of cards has 52 cards. What is the probability of drawing three aces in a row?

a. 1 in 52
b. 1 in 156
c. 1 in 5,525
d. 1 in 132,600

42. If $ax^2 + by = 0$, which of the following must be true?

a. $ax^2 = by$
b. $ax^2 = \sqrt{by}$
c. $ax = b\sqrt{y}$
d. $ax^2 = -by$

43. In the graph shown below, what is the slope of a line that passes through the origin and will intercept the line $y = f(x)$ at the point where $y = 2$?

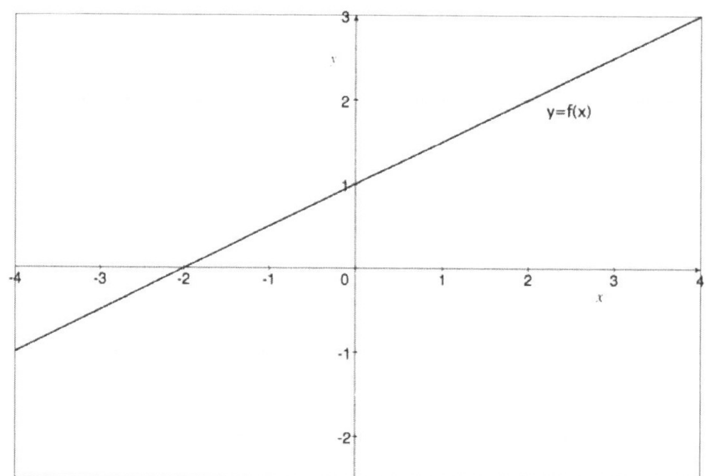

44. Which of the following completely describes the number of points in which two distinct quadratic functions can intersect?

a. 2
b. 0 or 1
c. 1 or 2
d. 0, 1, or 2

45. A satellite in a circular orbit revolves around Earth every 120 minutes. If Earth's radius is 4,000 miles at sea level, and the satellite's orbit is 400 miles above sea level, approximately what distance does the satellite travel in 40 minutes? Use 3.14 for π.

a. 4,121 miles
b. 4,400 miles
c. 8,000 miles
d. 9,211 miles

46. Which of the following equations best describes the straight line in the graph below? Note that a and b are non-zero constants.

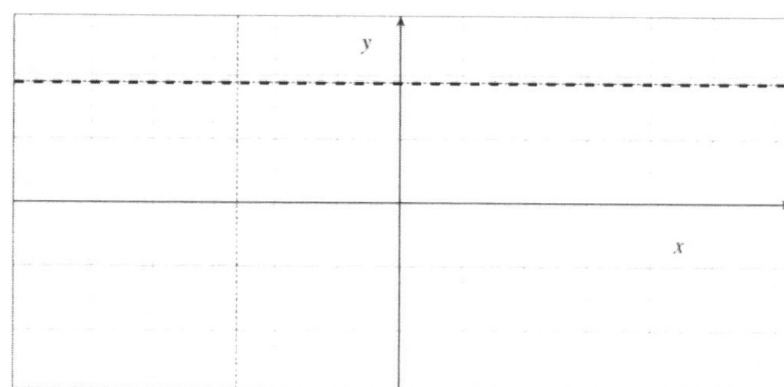

a. $y = x$
b. $x = a$
c. $y = ax + b$
d. $y = b$

47. Order the figures by increasing area:

Figure A, which is a circle with a diameter of 9 inches
Figure B, which is a circle with a radius of 5 inches
Figure C, which is a square with a side length of 7 inches

a. $B < C < A$
b. $B < A < C$
c. $C < B < A$
d. $C < A < B$

Refer to the following for questions 48–49:

A ticket agency finds that demand for tickets for a concert in a 25,000-seat stadium falls if the price is raised. The number of tickets sold, N, varies with the dollar price, p, according to the relationship $N = 25{,}000 - 0.1p^2$.

48. What is the lowest price at which they will sell no tickets at all?

a. \$10
b. \$25
c. \$50
d. \$500

49. No matter how many tickets are sold, the cost of putting on a concert is \$500,000. Which of the following equations can be used to calculate the profit Q made for any ticket price?

a. $Q = 25{,}000p - 0.1p^3$
b. $Q = 25{,}000p - 0.1p^3 - 500{,}000$
c. $Q = 25{,}000p - 0.1p^3 - 500{,}000p$
d. $Q = p(25{,}000 - 0.1p) - 500{,}000$

50. In the system of equations below, what is a possible value of y?

$$x^2 + y^2 = 24$$

$$2x^2 + 3y^2 = 52$$

a. 2
b. 3
c. 4
d. $2\sqrt{7}$

51. Which of the following pairs of shapes may tessellate a plane?

a. Regular pentagons and squares
b. Regular pentagons and equilateral triangles
c. Equilateral triangles and regular hexagons
d. Regular octagons and equilateral triangles

52. Which of the following statements is true?

a. A number is divisible by 3 if the sum of the digits is divisible by 3.
b. A number is divisible by 4 if the last digit is divisible by 2.
c. A number is divisible by 7 if the sum of the digits is divisible by 7.
d. A number is divisible by 6 if the sum of the last two digits is divisible by 6.

53. Hannah spends at least \$16 on 4 packages of coffee. Which of the following expresses this relationship in terms of the cost of a package of coffee, p?

a. $16 \geq 4p$
b. $16 < 4p$
c. $16 > 4p$
d. $16 \leq 4p$

54. Ms. Elliott asks her fifth-grade students, "Do you prefer chocolate or vanilla ice cream?" If the probability of her students preferring chocolate ice cream is 0.6, what is the probability of her students preferring vanilla ice cream?

a. 0.6
b. 0.4
c. 0.3
d. 0.5

55. Given this stem-and-leaf plot, what are the mean and median values?

Stem	Leaf
1	6 8
2	0 1
3	4
4	5 9

a. Mean = 28 and median = 20
b. Mean = 29 and median = 20
c. Mean = 29 and median = 21
d. Mean = 28 and median = 21

Science

Refer to the following for questions 1–6:

Pollutants typically enter seawater at point sources, such as sewage discharge pipes or factory waste outlets. Then, they may be spread over a wide area by wave action and currents. The rate of this dispersal depends upon a number of factors, including depth, temperature, and the speed of the currents. Chemical pollutants often attach themselves to small particles of sediment, so studying the dispersal of sediment can help in understanding how pollution spreads.

In a study of this type, a team of scientists lowered screened collection vessels to various depths to collect particles of different sizes. This gave them an idea of the size distribution of particles at each depth. Figure A shows the results for six different sites (ND, NS, MD, MS, SD, and SS). The particle size is plotted in phi units, which is a logarithmic scale used to measure grain sizes of sand and gravel. The 0 point of the scale is a grain size of 1 millimeter, and an increase of 1 in phi number corresponds to a decrease in grain size by a factor of 0.5. Therefore, 1 phi unit is a grain size of 0.5 mm, 2 phi units is 0.25 mm, and so on; in the other direction, -1 phi unit corresponds to a grain size of 2 mm and -2 phi units to 4 mm.

Grains of different size are carried at different rates by the currents in the water. The study also measured current speed and direction, as well as pressure and temperature at different depths, for a period of several months. The results were used in a computer modeling program to predict the total transport of sediments both along the shore (north-south) and perpendicular to it (east-west). Figure B shows the program's calculation of the distance particles would have been transported during the study period. The abbreviation *mab* in the figure stands for "meters above bottom."

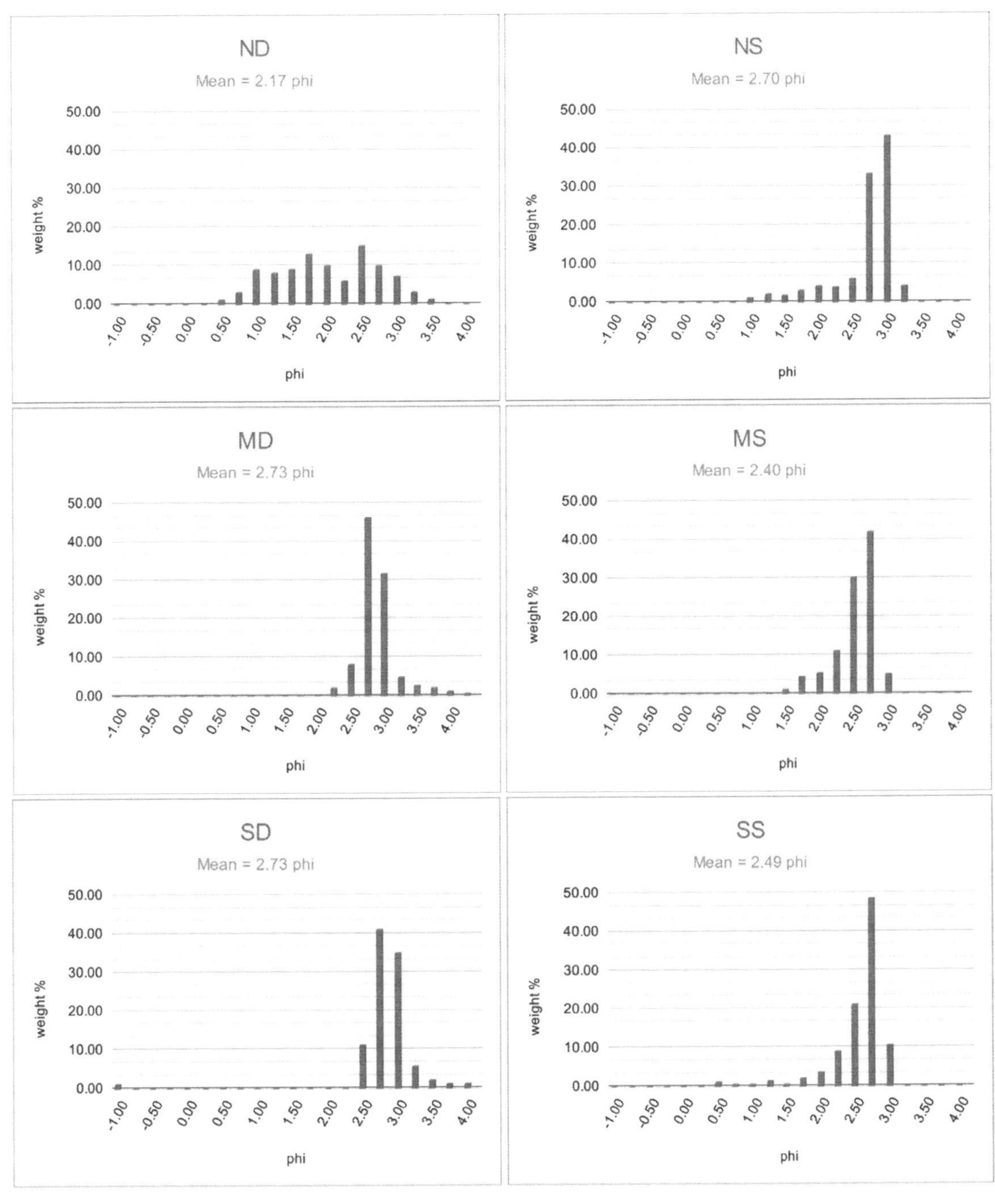

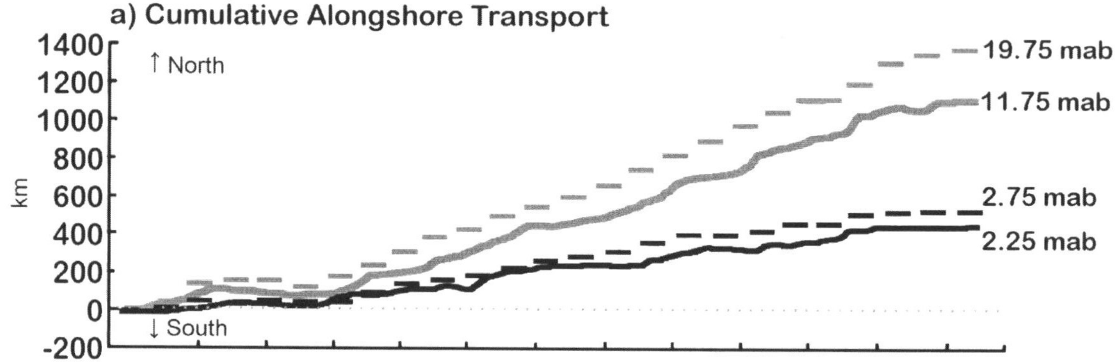

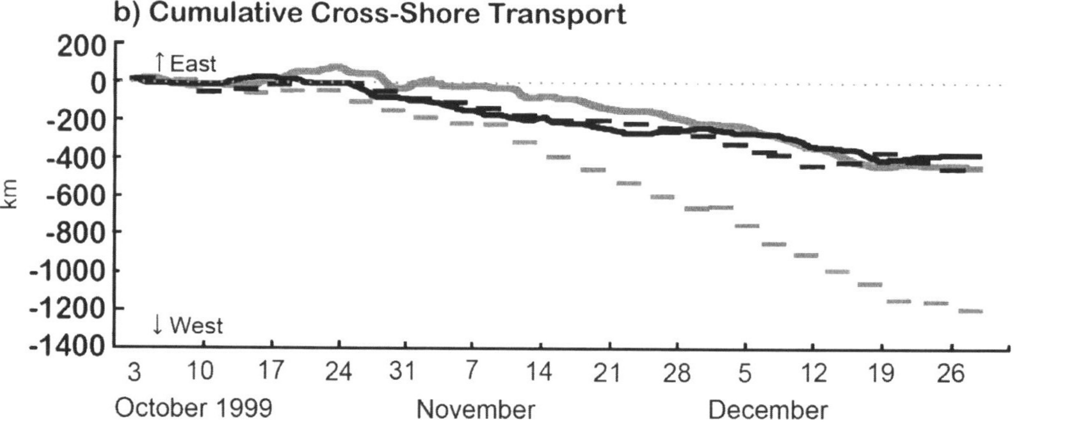

1. Which of the following sites was found to have the smallest average particle size?

a. ND
b. NS
c. MD
d. MS

2. With the exception of a few outliers, all of the phi values were in the range 1.0 to 4.0. This means that:

a. All particles studied were smaller than 0.5 mm.
b. All particles studied were between 1.0 and 4.0 mm.
c. No screens larger than 4.0 m were used in the study.
d. All particles were larger than 0.5 mm.

3. For which site is it LEAST true that the mean particle size represents the entire population?

a. ND
b. NS
c. MD
d. MS

4. What particle size corresponds to a phi value of –3?

a. 2 mm
b. 0.5 mm
c. 0.0625 mm
d. 8 mm

5. In Figure B, the absolute value of the slope of the curves corresponds to:

a. The speed of transport
b. The size of the particles
c. The phi value
d. The depth

6. The data indicate that along a north-south axis:

a. Transport is faster in deeper waters.
b. Transport is faster in shallower waters.
c. Transport is the same at all depths.
d. Transport is fastest at middle depths.

Refer to the following for questions 7–9:

Of the 4,000 species of frogs in the world, 427 are found in the Amazon rainforest. The Amazon rainforest is in South America, covering parts of Brazil, Peru, Colombia, and other countries. The climate is rainy, hot, and humid, which makes the area a perfect location for many species.

One type of frog found in the Amazon is the giant cane toad. This large toad is gray, yellow, or brown with dry and warty textured skin. In addition to living in the Amazon rainforest, this toad has been introduced to various other regions worldwide. The giant cane toad is primarily active during the night. It is omnivorous, but its preference is to feed on small animals and insects. The name *cane toad* arose from the use of these toads to eliminate sugarcane pests. The giant cane toad secretes a fluid from its skin that is highly toxic to most animals. If an animal catches a giant cane toad in its mouth, that animal can die from the highly toxic poison. The toxin can be irritating to humans. The giant cane toad also excretes white venom from its back.

Another type of frog found in the Amazon is the poison dart frog. These frogs are known for their bright colors, usually orange, red, or green. These small frogs are active during the day rather than at night. They are usually found on the rainforest floor. The poison dart frog feeds on small arthropods and insects. Poison dart frogs, as their name suggests, excrete a poison through their skin that is potent enough to kill an adult human. The name arose from the practice of a nearby indigenous people who would cover the ends of their darts in the poison from these frogs.

7. Select the answer that best describes a logical conclusion that could be made from the passage above.

a. Poisonous frogs can be found in different sizes and colors.
b. Poisonous frogs are located in areas where humans and other animals will not encounter them.
c. Poisonous frogs all have bright colors so humans and other animals know to avoid them.
d. Poisonous frogs tend to be very small so animals can avoid them more easily.

8. Based on the passage, which statement is true?

a. The poison dart frog and the giant cane toad have both been used for the advantage of humans.
b. The poison dart frog and the giant cane toad are both endangered species.
c. The poison dart frog and the giant cane toad both excrete toxins that cause death in humans and other animals.
d. The poison dart frog and the giant cane toad are both herbivores.

9. The northern glass frog is another frog that can be found in the Amazon rainforest. Like the giant cane toad, this frog is nocturnal. Which of the following best describes what *nocturnal* means?

a. The northern glass frog is mainly active at night.
b. The northern glass frog is active during the day and inactive at night.
c. The northern glass frog is mainly active during twilight.
d. The northern glass frog is active during both day and night.

Refer to the following for questions 10–11:

The relative position that an organism occupies within a food chain or food web is called its trophic level. An organism's trophic level is based on how it obtains its energy. All food chains or food webs have at least three trophic levels, with the primary producer at the lowest level and the top consumer at the highest level.

Primary producers are usually plants, algae, or phytoplankton, and they get their energy from the sun. These primary producers are considered trophic level 1, and they perform photosynthesis to create their own food supply. The organisms at trophic level 1 are food for the next trophic level.

Primary consumers form trophic level 2. These organisms are herbivores. They feed on the primary producers that capture energy from the sun through photosynthesis. Examples of primary consumers include cows, sheep, mice, and grasshoppers.

Secondary consumers form trophic level 3. These organisms are carnivores, and they feed on the primary consumers. Examples of secondary consumers include snakes, foxes, and lions. In a marine ecosystem, any animal that consumes zooplankton is a secondary consumer. Animals that eat zooplankton include jellyfish, crabs, and some whales.

Animals can be on more than one level in a food web. Some secondary consumers are omnivores. Omnivores feed on both primary producers and primary consumers. This means that omnivores are also primary consumers. For example, grizzly bears are omnivores that eat berries (primary producers) and salmon (primary consumers), so they can be considered both primary consumers (level 2) and secondary consumers (level 3).

Many food chains have tertiary consumers, on trophic level 4, who consume secondary consumers. Some food chains or webs have a fifth trophic level of quaternary consumers. There are even cases of food webs with six levels.

At the top of a food chain are apex predators, which do not have natural predators of their own. Apex predators are usually on trophic level 3, 4, or 5, depending on the food web. Lions, wolves, and sharks are examples of apex predators. Through predation, apex predators keep the populations of the lower trophic levels under control.

10. If an apex predator population were to disappear, which of the following is a likely outcome for the ecosystem?

a. The health of the overall ecosystem would improve.
b. There would be no impact on the ecosystem.
c. Their prey species would experience a population explosion and lack enough food to eat.
d. Any carnivores in the lower trophic levels would become herbivores.

11. Krill are small crustaceans that feed on zooplankton, and they are preyed upon by some fish and whales. Which trophic level do krill belong to?

a. Primary consumer
b. Secondary consumer
c. Tertiary consumer
d. Apex predator

Refer to the following for questions 12–17:

A *standing wave* occurs when a medium is vibrated at just the right frequency so that waves reflected off a barrier overlap (constructively interfere) with the original waves, building up into larger waves that remain in fixed positions. For example, it is the standing waves on a violin or piano string that produce the sounds that we hear from them.

A student wants to experiment with standing waves in a string. The student connects one end of the string to a wave driver, a device that oscillates vertically at an adjustable frequency. The student runs the other end over a pulley and ties it to a hanging weight, which provides the tension in the string. See the diagram below.

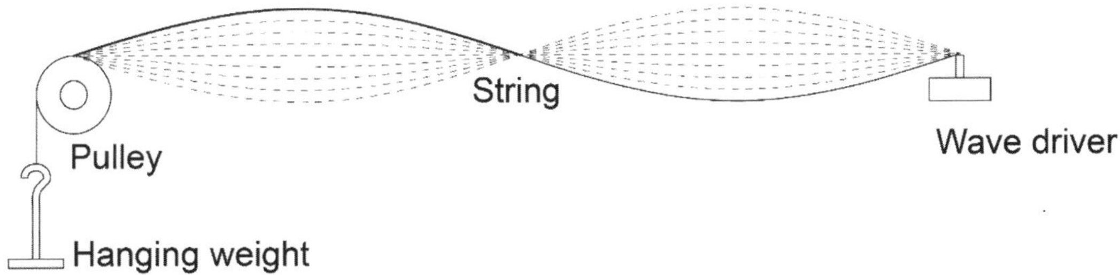

Study 1

The student first uses a fixed amount of weight on the string and measures the frequency at which a different number of standing waves appear in the string. (The diagram above shows two standing waves.) The student obtains the following data:

Table 1

Trial	Mass of hanging weight (g)	Frequency (Hz)	Number of waves
1	500	30	1
2	500	63	2
3	500	89	3
4	500	124	4
5	500	149	5

Study 2

The student then decides to investigate the dependence of the frequency on the tension in the string. This time the student varies the tension in the string by changing the mass of the hanging weight and measures the frequency that generates two standing waves. The student obtains the following data:

Table 2

Trial	Mass of hanging weight (g)	Frequency (Hz)	Number of waves
6	500	63	2
7	600	68	2
8	700	72	2
9	800	79	2
10	900	83	2
11	1,000	88	2

12. According to the student's data, which sentence MOST accurately describes the relationship between the frequency of the standing waves and the tension in the string?

a. They are directly proportional.
b. They are inversely proportional.
c. They are positively correlated but not directly proportional.
d. They are negatively correlated but not inversely proportional.

13. Suppose that the student wanted to check the dependence of the frequency on other variables. Which would be the BEST choice for another quantity to use as the independent variable?

a. The radius of the pulley
b. The length of the string
c. The frequency of the wave generator
d. The speed of the wave in the string

14. In the analysis, the student decides to calculate the tension of the string. Reasoning that the tension should be equal to the force of gravity on the hanging weight, the student multiplies the mass of the hanging weight in Study 1 by the acceleration of gravity, $9.8\ m/s^2$, to get 4,900 N. What is wrong with this calculation?

a. The student forgot to convert the mass to kilograms.
b. The student forgot to take into account the mass of the string.
c. The student should have divided the mass by $9.8\ m/s^2$, not multiplied.
d. Because the weight pulls on only one end of the string, the value should be halved.

15. Based on the student's data, about what frequency would you expect to generate four standing waves if the mass of the hanging weight was 800 g?

a. 40 Hz
b. 80 Hz
c. 160 Hz
d. 320 Hz

16. Suppose the student wants to plot a graph of the results from Study 2. What quantity would be the best choice to go on the x-axis of the graph?

a. The trial number
b. The mass of the hanging weight
c. The frequency of the wave driver
d. The number of standing waves

17. What is likely to be the largest source of error in the student's measurements?

a. Variation in the mass of the string between trials
b. Interference due to vibration of the surroundings
c. Uncertainty in counting the number of standing waves
d. Uncertainty in finding the exact frequencies corresponding to specific numbers of standing waves

Refer to the following for questions 18–19:

Malik is conducting an experiment to find out the effect of different liquids on plant growth. He is using three plants: basil, marigold, and aloe. The liquids for the experiment are lemon juice mixed with tap water, milk mixed with tap water, and vinegar mixed with tap water. To conduct the experiment, Malik applies 4 oz of lemon juice mixed with tap water to the basil plant, 4 oz of milk mixed with tap water to the marigold, and 4 oz of vinegar mixed with tap water to the aloe plant every other day. He records plant growth, in centimeters, for a total of six weeks. He also records the number of leaves on each plant, as well as any other visible changes such as discoloration.

18. Which of the following aspects of the experimental design creates a confounding variable?

a. The use of three different types of plants
b. The duration of recording plant growth
c. The measurement the plant growth in centimeters
d. The application of liquid every other day

19. Which of the following could be included in the experiment to strengthen the design and provide a baseline for the results?

a. The measurement of the pH values of the liquids
b. Variations in the depth of soil for each plant
c. The measurement of plant growth in inches instead of centimeters
d. The addition of a control group

Refer to the following for questions 20–21:

Liz is examining the plant growth of two different plant species under controlled conditions. After collecting data, she found that plant A has a 50% chance of sprouting within the first 14 days after planting, and plant B has a 70% chance of sprouting within the first 14 days after planting.

20. If Liz plants one of each type of seed, what is the probability that both plants will sprout within the first 14 days?

a. 35%
b. 75%
c. 60%
d. 45%

21. What is the probability that neither of the plants will sprout within the first 14 days?

a. 70%
b. 65%
c. 40%
d. 15%

Refer to the following for questions 22–23:

Jaden notices that the milkweed plants in his front yard, where there are no other large plants, grow taller than the milkweed plants in his back yard, where there are also several shade trees. He investigates the link between plant growth and sunlight, and he reads about photosynthesis, which powers energy production and fuels cellular growth in plants. He then sets up a test at school with two identical groups of milkweeds. Group A is placed in a location that receives full sun, and Group B is placed in a shady location nearby. After several weeks of recording plant growth, Jaden finds that the plants in Group A have grown taller than the plants in Group B.

22. Which of the following steps of the scientific process is missing from this scenario?

a. Data collection
b. Hypothesis
c. Research
d. Experiment

23. Which of the following is a reasonable conclusion for Jaden to reach after his experiment?

a. Sunlight negatively affects the growth of milkweed.
b. Shade is inappropriate for all types of plants.
c. Photosynthesis does not affect plant growth.
d. Sunlight positively affects the growth of milkweed.

Refer to the following for questions 24–26:

Gravity is a force that pulls on objects. According to Newton's universal law of gravitation, both mass and proximity positively affect gravitational pull. The Moon's gravitational pull is strong enough to displace the oceans on Earth. It causes the ocean to bulge on both the side closest and the side farthest away from the Moon. These bulges result in high tides. Every location on Earth experiences two high tides and two low tides per day. The highest tides, called spring tides, occur twice a month.

The Sun also creates tidal forces on Earth's oceans. These solar tides are about half of the size of lunar tides. When the Earth, the Moon, and the Sun are aligned, extra-high tides and extra-low tides are created by this alignment. When these three bodies are at right angles to one another, the Sun partly cancels out the effects of the lunar tide, resulting in moderate tides called neap tides.

24. Imagine that the Moon suddenly had a much larger mass. Which of the following would likely be a result of the Moon's increased mass?

a. It would have no effect on tides.
b. It would cause more extreme tides due to a higher gravitational pull.
c. The Earth would no longer experience high tides.
d. The Sun would stop affecting the tidal patterns on Earth.

25. Which of the following best describes the concept of gravitational pull?

a. A force that adds mass to any object
b. A force that prevents objects from decelerating
c. A force of attraction that draws two objects together
d. A force that mainly affects solid objects

26. Which of the following conclusions could be made based on the passage?

a. Spring tides are caused when the Earth, Moon, and Sun align.
b. The Sun exerts a higher gravitational pull on Earth than the Moon does.
c. The same side of the Earth is always facing the Moon.
d. Neap tides are higher than spring tides.

Refer to the following for questions 27–28:

This chart shows the distance each planet is from the Sun, in astronomical units (AU).

Planet	Distance from Sun (Astronomical Units)
Mercury	0.38
Venus	0.72
Earth	1
Mars	1.52
Jupiter	5.2
Saturn	9.58
Uranus	19.14
Neptune	30.2

27. If light takes 8.5 minutes to travel from the Sun to Earth, how long would it take for light to travel from the Sun to Saturn?

a. 6.1 minutes
b. 1.36 hours
c. 2.7 hours
d. 12.9 minutes

28. It takes 7.2 minutes for light to travel from the Sun to a large asteroid that is traveling in an orbit between the orbits of two planets. Which two planets is the asteroid between?

a. Mars and Jupiter
b. Earth and Mars
c. Venus and Earth
d. Mercury and Venus

Refer to the following for questions 29–32:

The Respiratory System

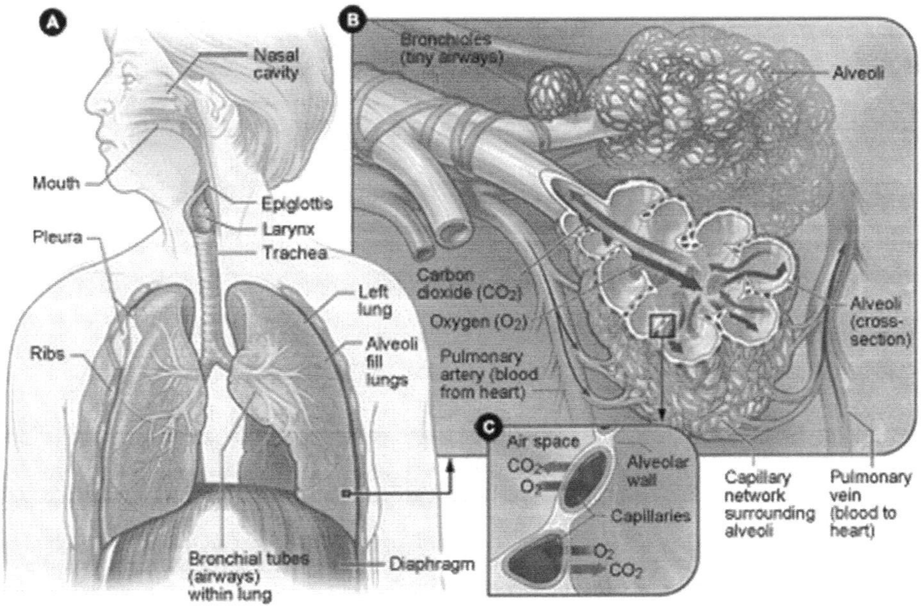

The human body's respiratory system works with the circulatory system to provide oxygen to the body and to remove waste products of metabolism. The respiratory system is made up of several components as shown in the diagram. The process includes both internal and external respiration. External respiration involves the processes through which the body takes in oxygen-rich air and delivers it to the alveoli. Internal respiration involves the processes that take place at a cellular level, where red blood cells carry oxygen to other cells around the body. The oxygen is used during cellular respiration, and the red blood cells transport waste products back to the lungs. The respiratory process is important for the production of energy and enables the tissues and cells throughout the body to function properly.

29. Which of the following is the correct sequence of components used during respiration?

a. Alveoli – nose and mouth – larynx – trachea – bronchioles
b. Larynx – alveoli – trachea – nose and mouth – bronchioles
c. Trachea – bronchioles – nose and mouth – larynx – alveoli
d. Nose and mouth – larynx – trachea – bronchioles – alveoli

30. Which of the following components is involved in internal respiration?

a. Larynx
b. Red blood cells
c. Trachea
d. Bronchioles

31. Which of the following is the waste product that is removed from the body by the process of respiration?

a. Carbon dioxide
b. Oxygen
c. Alveoli
d. Pharynx

32. Which of the following is the source of the red blood cells used during internal respiration?

a. Bronchioles
b. Pulmonary artery
c. Pulmonary vein
d. Alveolar wall

Refer to the following for questions 33–37:

Titration is a method of assessing the concentration of a solution by slowly adding a second solution that is known to react with the first solution at particular levels of relative concentration. The solution that is added is called the *titrant*; the original solution to which it is added is called the *titrand*. By measuring the amount of titrant that has been added when the reaction occurs, the concentration of the titrand can be calculated. To facilitate this measurement, the titrant is usually added with an instrument called a burette that can release the titrant one drop at a time, as shown in the diagram below.

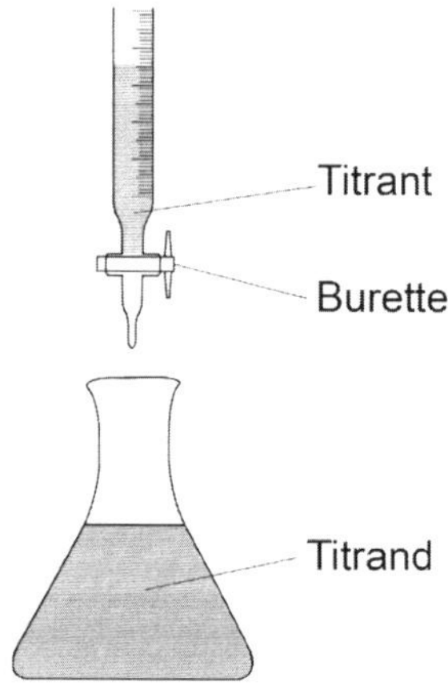

One common application of titration is *acid-base titration*: the titrant is acidic and the titrand basic, or vice versa. As the titrant is added, the pH of the solution changes. This change in pH can be plotted in a graph called a *titration curve*.

A student performs a titration with particular chemicals and obtains the titration curve shown below.

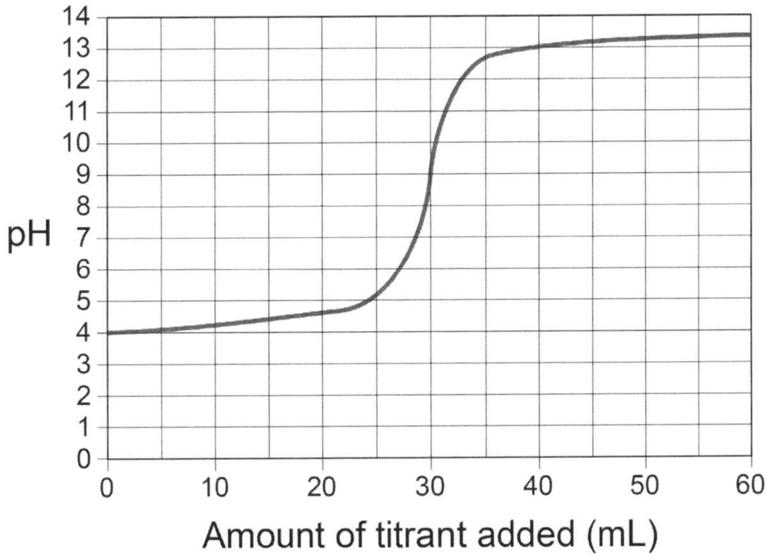

33. Judging by the titration curve, are the titrant and the titrand of this titration acidic or basic?

a. Both are acidic.
b. Both are basic.
c. The titrant is acidic; the titrand is basic.
d. The titrant is basic; the titrand is acidic.

34. Which sentence MOST accurately describes the rate of increase of the pH as more titrant is added?

a. The rate of increase continually rises.
b. The rate of increase continually falls.
c. The rate of increase first rises then falls.
d. The rate of increase first falls then rises.

35. Suppose a titration was performed with the same titrant but a more concentrated titrand. Which graph best matches what you would expect the titration curve to look like?

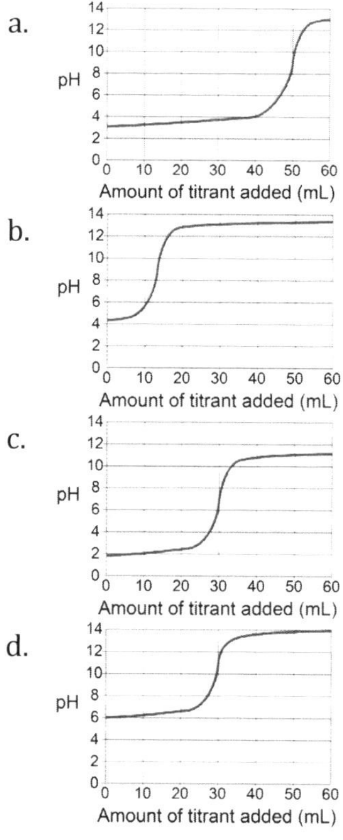

36. The student has a second sample of the titrand solution and wants to check that it has the same concentration as the first. Instead of measuring the pH at every step and generating a full titration curve, the student decides to use an indicator solution—a substance that changes color at a particular pH range—and verify that the solution does reach the indicated pH when the expected amount of titrant is added.

The table below lists the characteristics of four common indicators.

Indicator	Color change	pH range of color change
Bromothymol blue	Yellow → Blue	6.0 – 7.6
Litmus	Red → Blue	4.5 – 8.3
Methyl orange	Red → Yellow	3.1 – 4.4
Phenolphthalein	Colorless → Pink	8.3 – 10.0

Which indicator would be the best choice for the student to use?

a. Bromothymol blue
b. Litmus
c. Methyl orange
d. Phenolphthalein

37. Where should the indicator be initially added?

a. To the titrand
b. To the titrant
c. To both the titrand and the titrant
d. To neither until after the titration is completed

Refer to the following for questions 38–42:

Joe is reading about plant germination, and he learns that some seeds germinate more readily when they are cold stratified. After examining the process of cold stratification, he designs an experiment to see how the cold stratification of milkweed seeds affects their germination. He places 20 seeds on a damp paper towel and places them in a plastic bag in the refrigerator. After one month, he plants these 20 seeds in seed starting soil and 20 milkweed seeds that were not cold stratified in the same seed starting soil. For sun exposure, Joe places the cold-stratified seeds in an east facing window and the regular seeds in a south facing window. The indoor room temperature is kept at a constant 75 °F. He waters the seeds regularly and waits for the seeds to sprout. He records the results each day after the first seed sprouts, noting which seeds sprout from the cold-stratified seeds and from the regular seeds. After recording his results for several weeks, he concludes that the cold-stratified milkweed seeds germinate more readily than those that were not.

38. Which of the following would be an appropriate hypothesis for this experiment?

a. I think cold stratification is a good idea.
b. Cold stratification can make seeds germinate more readily.
c. If I cold stratify milkweed seeds, they will germinate more readily than seeds that were not cold stratified.
d. I will plant the seeds at the same time and see which ones germinate first.

39. Which of the following is a potential flaw in the design of this experiment?

a. Publication bias
b. Confounding variable
c. Insufficient randomization
d. Excessive sample size

40. Which of the following are the independent and dependent variables in this experiment?

a. Independent: cold stratification; dependent: plant germination
b. Independent: room temperature; dependent: cold stratification
c. Independent: amount of water; dependent: plant germination
d. Independent: soil type; dependent: amount of water

41. Which of the following would strengthen the design of this experiment?

a. Recording plant growth weekly
b. Measuring the amount of water used
c. Using a different type of soil for each set of seeds
d. Using a smaller sample size

42. Which of the following best defines the term *cold stratification*?

a. Saving seeds in the freezer to plant outside next spring
b. Germinating seeds in a plastic bag instead of soil
c. Placing seeds in a cold, dark place to keep them from germinating
d. Exposing seeds to moist, cold conditions to encourage germination

Refer to the following for questions 43–48:

The *specific heat* of a substance is a measurement of the amount of thermal energy needed to change the temperature of the substance—the higher the specific heat, the more energy it takes to raise a given mass of the substance by 1 degree Celsius. Specific heat can be calculated by measuring the amount of energy gained or lost as the substance heats up or cools down, a process known as *calorimetry*.

One way to perform calorimetry of an unknown solid is as follows: A sample of the solid is heated up to a known temperature and placed in an insulated container full of water at a lower temperature. Heat flows from the sample to the water, cooling the solid and warming the water until they are both at the same temperature and the system has reached equilibrium. This final temperature is measured. Because the specific heat of water is known, we can calculate the amount of heat that the water gained. This must be equal to the amount of heat lost by the solid, allowing us to calculate the solid's specific heat.

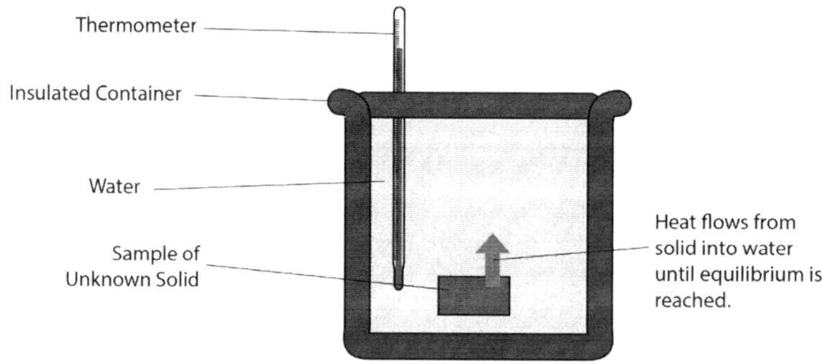

A student wishes to measure the specific heat of an unknown metal and performs two sets of trials to do so using the process described above. In each trial, the student immerses the substance in 2.00 kg of water initially at 20.0 °C.

Study 1

In the first set of trials, the student varies the initial temperature of the unknown metal.

Table 1

Trial	Mass of metal (g)	Initial temperature of metal (°C)	Final temperature of system (°C)
1	400	80	21.1
2	400	100	21.5
3	400	120	21.8
4	400	160	22.5
5	400	200	23.3

Study 2

The student then performed another set of five trials in which he or she kept the initial temperature constant but used pieces of metal of different masses:

Table 2

Trial	Mass of metal (g)	Initial temperature of metal (°C)	Final temperature of system (°C)
6	200	160	21.3
7	400	160	22.5
8	600	160	23.8
9	800	160	25.0
10	1,000	160	26.2

43. Which graph best shows the relationship between the initial temperature of the metal sample and the final temperature in the first set of trials?

a. 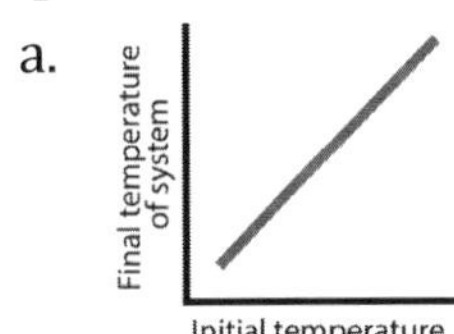

b. 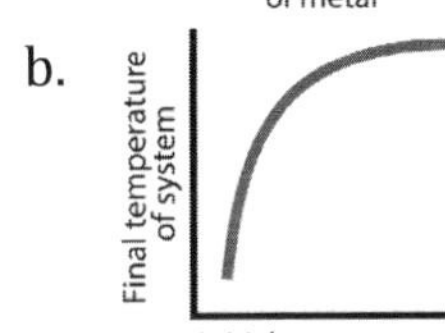

c. 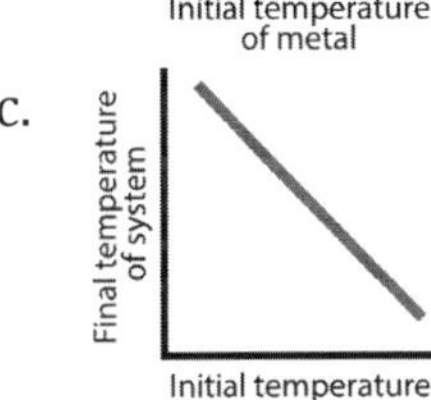

d. 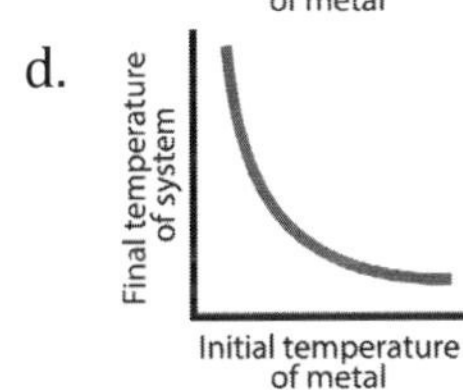

44. The student produces a graph of the final temperature versus the mass of the metal in the second set of trials. The graph looks like this:

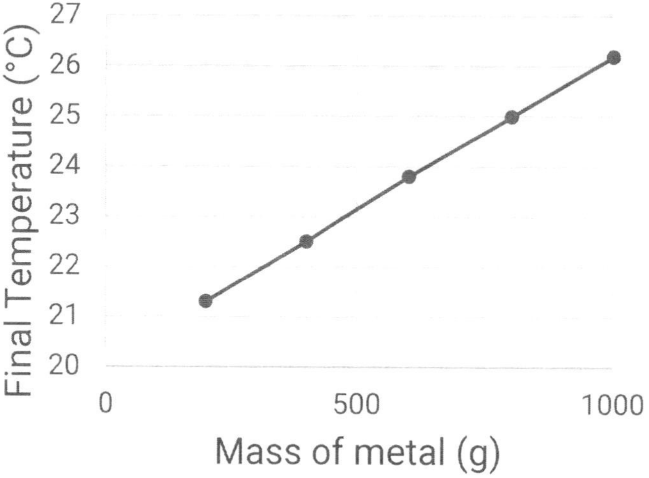

How would this graph look different if the student had measured the temperature in kelvin instead of degrees Celsius?

a. The graph would be reflected vertically.
b. The graph would be reflected horizontally.
c. The graph would have the same shape, but the x-axis would be labeled differently.
d. The graph would have the same shape, but the y-axis would be labeled differently.

45. In principle, the results of a single trial would have been sufficient to calculate the specific heat of the metal. What is an advantage of performing multiple trials?

a. It reduces the effects of random error.
b. It reduces the effects of systematic error.
c. As the system accommodates, later trials become more accurate.
d. There is no advantage; the student should only have performed a single trial.

46. Which of the student's trials involved exactly the same conditions?

a. 1 and 6
b. 2 and 7
c. 4 and 7
d. 4 and 9

47. The passage says that the procedure must be done with an insulated container. What would go wrong if a non-insulated container was used?

a. Heat transfer would not occur, and the metal and water would each remain at their original temperatures.
b. Heat would be exchanged with the environment, and the system would stabilize at the temperature of its surroundings.
c. Heat would be continually lost to the environment, and the system would stabilize at a temperature below that of its surroundings.
d. The final temperature of the system would not stabilize but would continually oscillate between extremes.

48. The specific heat of saltwater is lower than the specific heat of pure water. If the experiment had been done with saltwater instead of pure water, how would you expect the final temperatures to change?

a. The final temperatures would be higher.
b. The final temperatures would be lower.
c. The final temperatures would not change.
d. It would not have been possible to carry out the procedure with saltwater.

Refer to the following for questions 49–50:

This chart shows the inheritance patterns for ABO blood groups. One of three alleles is inherited from each parent, which results in four possible phenotypes, or blood types.

Father

Mother	A	B	O
A	A	AB	A
B	AB	B	B
O	A	B	O

49. If a child has type B blood, which of the following might describe the alleles inherited from each parent?

a. A from the father and B from the mother
b. O from the father and O from the mother
c. B from the father and O from the mother
d. B from the father and A from the mother

50. Which of the following conclusions can be made from the data in the chart?

a. AB can sometimes include O alleles.
b. A is a common blood type.
c. Very few people receive O alleles.
d. The A and B alleles are dominant over O.

Refer to the following for questions 51–53:

A scientist obtained 10 cuttings from a rare type of plant and wants to check the growth rate of those 10 cuttings. She plants the cuttings in potting soil and waters the cuttings regularly. The cuttings are kept in a room with a constant temperature and partial sunlight. The results of the growth are shown in the chart.

Week	Plant Growth (cm)
1	0.3
2	1.4
3	1.7
4	2
5	5
6	1.9
7	6.1

51. Which of the following would be a potential benefit of increasing the duration of the experiment from 7 weeks to 20 weeks?

a. Finding the optimal temperature for plant growth
b. Increasing the possibility of error in the experiment
c. Increasing the overall cost of the experiment
d. Determining whether there are multiple spikes in plant growth

52. Which of the following would increase the reliability of the data from this experiment?

a. Controlling the environment
b. Checking growth at regular intervals
c. Increasing the sample size
d. Planting in the same conditions

53. Which of the following measures of central tendency would best predict how much a larger sample of the same rare plant cuttings would grow each week over a span of 7 weeks?

a. Mean and median
b. Median and mode
c. Mode only
d. Median only

Refer to the following for questions 54–56:

Global warming is a phenomenon that scientists attribute to human activity. Energy from the Sun sustains life on Earth. About half of the heat energy from the Sun passes through the Earth's atmosphere to reach the surface. Gasses known as greenhouse gasses trap heat near the Earth's surface. This helps to maintain a stable and warm atmosphere so that the Earth can sustain life, but an increase in carbon dioxide over the last century has been trapping extra heat near the Earth's surface and causing the temperature to slowly rise. This is known as the greenhouse effect.

The Earth's atmosphere is made up of about 78% nitrogen and 21% oxygen. It also contains other gases, including hydrogen, neon, and carbon dioxide, or CO_2. CO_2 is a greenhouse gas that is released into the atmosphere through natural processes, including animals exhaling CO_2 and volcanic activity, and the burning of natural gas, coal, and oil. Methane (CH_4) is another greenhouse gas that contributes to the greenhouse effect. It comes from the breakdown of plant matter, as well as emissions from livestock during digestion. Another major source of methane is leaks from fossil fuel production. The greenhouse gas nitrous oxide (N_2O) is produced when soil is over-fertilized and when fossil fuels and vegetation are burned, and it is also emitted by soils in natural ecosystems. Chlorofluorocarbons, or CFCs, are greenhouse gas compounds that were used in spray can propellants and refrigerants. An international agreement now regulates the use of CFCs because of the damage they cause to the ozone layer.

54. How can global warming from carbon dioxide be attributed to human activity?

a. Humans have been raising more livestock over the last several years.
b. Humans have been burning an increasing amount of fuel over the past century.
c. Humans have been using more refrigerants to keep foods cold or frozen.
d. Humans have been increasing their fertilizer usage to grow more food.

55. Which of the following greenhouse gases has only an industrial origin?

a. CO_2
b. CH_4
c. N_2O
d. CFCs

56. Based on the passage, which of the following is most likely true?

a. Humans can change their contributions to global warming.
b. The temperature of the Earth will start to fall soon.
c. Farming rather than raising animals will solve the global warming issue.
d. The continued use of CFCs will have no effect on the ozone layer.

57. In ladybugs, there are two alleles for the gene for spot color: s for black spots, and S for red spots. SS and Ss result in a ladybug with red spots, and ss results in a ladybug with black spots.

If a population of 100 ladybugs includes 33 with an SS genotype, 38 with an Ss genotype, and 29 with an ss genotype, what percentage of those 100 ladybugs will have red spots?

a. 33%
b. 38%
c. 71%
d. 29%

58. Select the data chart that most accurately matches the graph shown below.

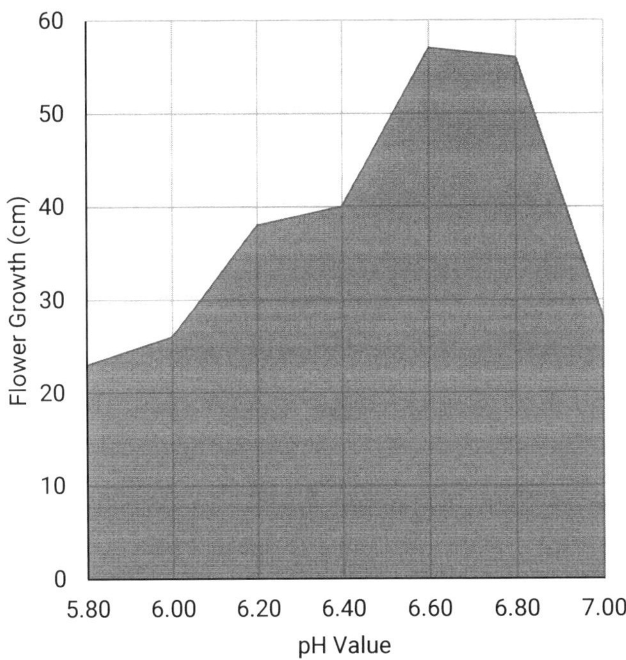

a.

pH Value	Flower Growth (cm)
23	5.8
36	6
38	6.2
40	6.4
57	6.6
56	6.8
28	7

c.

pH Value	Flower Growth (cm)
6	23
8	26
8.2	38
8.4	40
8.6	57
8.8	56
9	28

b.

pH Value	Flower Growth (cm)
5.8	33
6	46
6.2	48
6.4	50
6.6	67
6.8	66
7	38

d.

pH Value	Flower Growth (cm)
5.8	23
6	26
6.2	38
6.4	40
6.6	57
6.8	56
7	28

59. John is conducting an experiment to see how different amounts of fertilizer affect plant growth. He is conducting the experiment in a covered greenhouse, and two of his friends are assisting him.

Which of the following would be considered an independent variable in this experiment?

a. The number of people conducting the experiment
b. The amount of fertilizer used
c. The temperature of the air in the greenhouse
d. The weather outside of the greenhouse

60. A student is conducting a research project on the effects of a certain medication. The student discovered three research studies that report contradictory findings. Study A reports that the medication has been found to be ineffective compared to a placebo. Study B reports that the medication is only effective for people of a certain age range. Study C reports that the medication leads to an increased risk of gastrointestinal issues.

Which of the following best describes how the student can reconcile these findings?

a. Disregard Studies A and B and use the information from Study C to support his or her own findings.
b. Analyze the sample sizes, methodologies, and findings of all three studies to identify the factors that affected the outcomes.
c. Use the parts of each study that best support the conclusion that he or she is leading toward.
d. Disregard Study A, since the other studies show levels of effectiveness, and combine the findings of Studies B and C.

Social Studies

Refer to the following for questions 1–3:

The following is an excerpt from a speech about the nation's space effort given by President John F. Kennedy at Rice University in 1962.

"We set sail on this new sea because there is new knowledge to be gained, and new rights to be won, and they must be won and used for the progress of all people. For space science, like nuclear science and all technology, has no conscience of its own. Whether it will become a force for good or ill depends on man, and only if the United States occupies a position of pre-eminence can we help decide whether this new ocean will be a sea of peace or a new terrifying theater of war. I do not say that we should or will go unprotected against the hostile misuse of space any more than we go unprotected against the hostile use of land or sea, but I do say that space can be explored and mastered without feeding the fires of war, without repeating the mistakes that man has made in extending his writ around this globe of ours.

There is no strife, no prejudice, no national conflict in outer space as yet. Its hazards are hostile to us all. Its conquest deserves the best of all mankind, and its opportunity for peaceful cooperation may never come again. But why, some say, the moon? Why choose this as our goal? And they may well ask, why climb the highest mountain? Why, 35 years ago, fly the Atlantic? Why does Rice play Texas?

We choose to go to the moon. We choose to go to the moon in this decade and do the other things, not because they are easy, but because they are hard, because that

> goal will serve to organize and measure the best of our energies and skills, because that challenge is one that we are willing to accept, one we are unwilling to postpone, and one which we intend to win, and the others, too.
>
> It is for these reasons that I regard the decision last year to shift our efforts in space from low to high gear as among the most important decisions that will be made during my incumbency in the office of the Presidency."

1. One of Kennedy's strategies during his speech was to characterize space as a beckoning frontier. Which of the following phrases falls within this strategy?

a. "We choose to go to the moon in this decade and do the other things, not because they are easy..."
b. "There is no strife, no prejudice, no national conflict in outer space as yet."
c. "It is for these reasons that I regard the decision last year to shift our efforts in space from low to high gear..."
d. "Whether it will become a force for good or ill depends on man..."

2. Which of the following describes the purpose of Kennedy's repetition in this speech?

a. To explain that there is no real reason to travel to the Moon
b. To emphasize the presence of hazards in space
c. To highlight the urgency and importance of his message
d. To stress the concept that space travel is like mountain climbing

3. Kennedy used loaded language in his speech as a method of persuasion. Which of these phrases is an example of loaded language?

a. "For space science, like nuclear science and all technology, has no conscience of its own."
b. "...that challenge is one that we are willing to accept, one we are unwilling to postpone, and one which we intend to win..."
c. "There is no strife, no prejudice, no national conflict in outer space as yet."
d. "And they may well ask, why climb the highest mountain? Why, 35 years ago, fly the Atlantic?"

Refer to the following for questions 4–5:

This graph shows an increase of demand (D1 to D2) for the supply at the Island Coffee Company. In this graph, S represents supply.

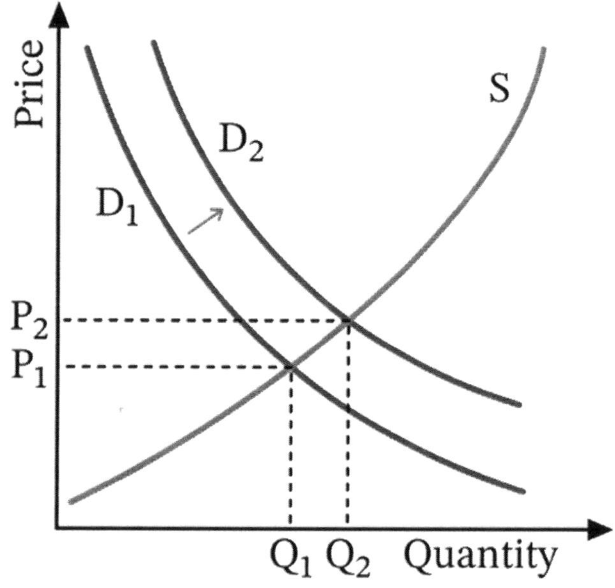

4. Which of the following is a result of the increased demand on the supply of coffee?

a. Price decreases with increased demand.
b. Quantity remains the same with increased demand.
c. Quantity decreases with increased demand.
d. Price increases with increased demand.

5. Which of the following could lead to an increase in supply while not affecting the price?

a. The company expands to a second manufacturing facility.
b. The company hires several new employees.
c. The company exchanges their equipment for new, more-efficient equipment.
d. The company switches to a certified organic supplier.

Refer to the following for questions 6–7:

The first map shows major cities in Canada, and the darker area on the second map indicates the high population around the Toronto area.

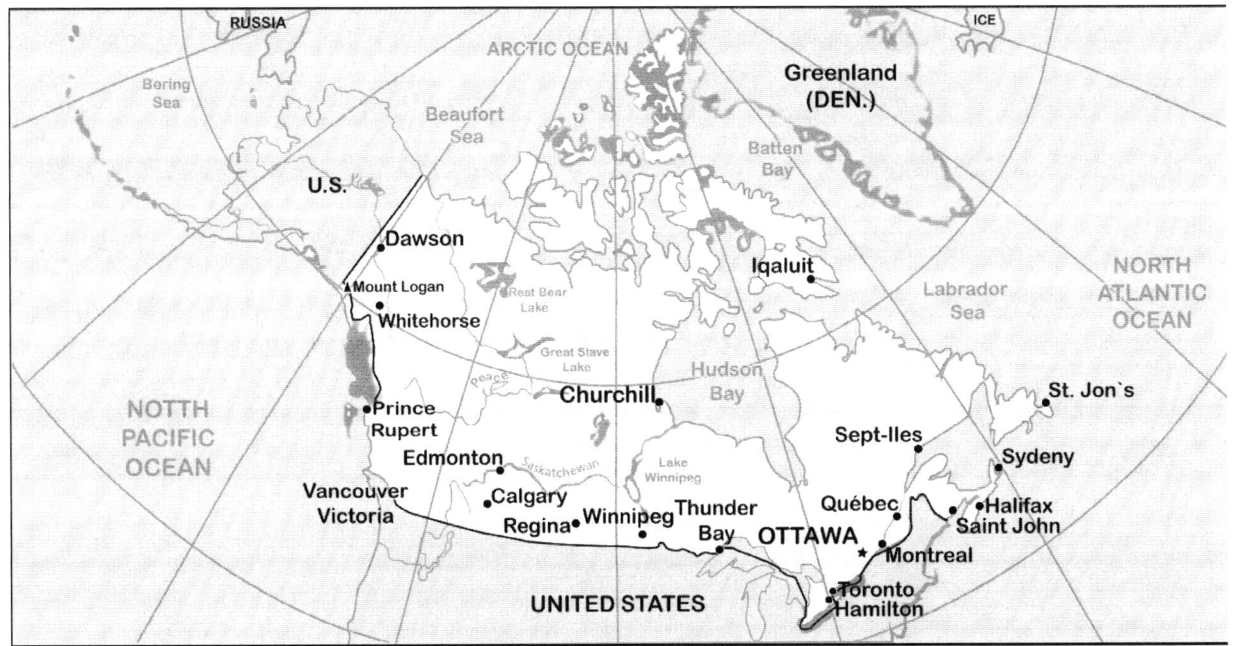

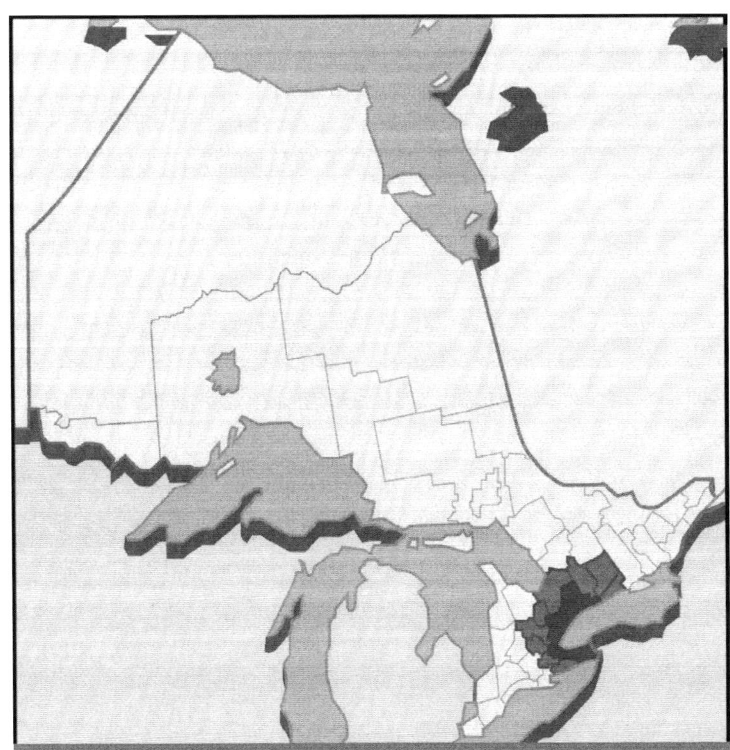

6. Approximately 26% of the population of Canada lives in the darker-colored region shown in the second map. Which of the following are likely reasons for this?

a. This area is easy to get to from the rest of Canada and has access to multiple lakes.
b. This area has ample space for expansion and can use nearby water for entertainment.
c. This area is in the far south of the country with a warmer climate and includes two large cities.
d. This area is close to multiple other countries and has direct ocean access.

7. Which of the following is a benefit of the locations of most of the cities shown on the map of Canada?

a. Warm climate
b. Ease of travel and trade
c. Proximity to each other
d. Access to borders of other countries

Refer to the following for questions 8–10:

The following is an excerpt from President Woodrow Wilson's speech to Congress on April 2, 1917.

> With a profound sense of the solemn and even tragical character of the step I am taking and of the grave responsibilities which it involves, but in unhesitating obedience to what I deem my constitutional duty, I advise that the Congress declare the recent course of the Imperial German government to be in fact nothing less than war against the government and people of the United States; that it formally accept the status of belligerent which has thus been thrust upon it; and that it take immediate steps, not only to put the country in a more thorough state of defense but also to exert all its power and employ all its resources to bring the government of the German Empire to terms and end the war.
>
> While we do these things, these deeply momentous things, let us be very clear, and make very clear to all the world, what our motives and our objects are. ...
>
> Our object now, as then, is to vindicate the principles of peace and justice in the life of the world as against selfish and autocratic power and to set up among the really free and self-governed peoples of the world such a concert of purpose and of action as will henceforth ensure the observance of those principles. Neutrality is no longer feasible or desirable where the peace of the world is involved and the freedom of its peoples, and the menace to that peace and freedom lies in the existence of autocratic governments backed by organized force which is controlled wholly by their will, not by the will of their people. We have seen the last of neutrality in such circumstances. We are at the beginning of an age in which it will be insisted that the same standards of conduct and of responsibility for wrong done shall be observed among nations and their governments that are observed among the individual citizens of civilized states.

The following is an excerpt from a New York Times *article describing President Wilson's speech to Congress:*

> Before an audience that cheered him as he has never been cheered in the Capitol in his life, the President cast in the lot of Americans unreservedly with the Allies and declared for a war that must not end until the issue between autocracy and

democracy has been fought out. He recited our injuries at Germany's hands, but he did not rest our cause on those; he went on from that point to range us with the Allies as a factor in an irrepressible conflict between the autocrat and the people. He showed that peace was impossible for the democracies of the world while this power remained on earth. "The world," he said, "must be made safe for democracy."

...

When he came to this part of his address the first big cheer he got was when, painting the battle of democracy and autocracy, and the difference between the two, he said that democracies "do not fill other countries with spies or set upon a course of intrigue" -and would have said more but for the cheering that split his sentence at that word.

8. What was the main purpose of President Wilson's speech?

a. To implore Americans to spread peace and justice to other countries
b. To convince Congress that America must go to war against Germany
c. To explain the stance of the US in the current political climate
d. To describe to Congress the standards of conduct in the US

9. Which of these words best describes the *New York Times'* coverage of President Wilson's speech?

a. Biased
b. Objective
c. Symbolic
d. Analytical

10. Which of the following is the most accurate comparison of President Wilson's speech excerpt and the *New York Times* article excerpt?

a. The purpose of the speech was to inform Congress, while the purpose of the article was to inform the American people.
b. The purpose of the speech was to entertain Congress, while the purpose of the article was to educate the American people.
c. The purpose of the speech was to persuade Congress, while the purpose of the article was to persuade the American people.
d. The purpose of the speech was to educate Congress, while the purpose of the article was to entertain the American people.

Refer to the following for questions 11–12:

"I DID NOT RAISE MY GIRL TO BE A VOTER"
SOPRANO SOLO WITH VOCIFEROUS SUPPORTING CHORUS OF MALE VOICES

11. Which of the following best characterizes the artist's opinion of the topic of this political cartoon?

a. Women should be allowed to vote.
b. Girls should not be raised to be voters.
c. Men should be in control of voting.
d. Labor practices should be controlled by men.

12. Which of the following is a conclusion that could be made from this cartoon?

a. Labor leaders support women's right to vote.
b. Women are in agreement with not being able to vote.
c. Political bosses should control both women's rights and labor practices.
d. If women were allowed to vote, they would vote against poor labor practices.

Refer to the following for questions 13–14:

Year	Number of Digital Video Game Users (in millions)	Number of Music Streaming Subscribers in US (in millions)
2017	145.28	198.6
2018	148.95	229.5
2019	153.85	304.9
2020	169.7	341
2021	176.11	400
2022	169.03	443

13. In this chart, the data for digital video game users and music streaming subscribers shows a mostly ____.

a. negative correlation
b. negative causation
c. positive correlation
d. positive causation

14. Using the data given for the number of music streaming subscribers, which of the following is the best measure of central tendency?

a. Median
b. Both mean and median
c. Both mean and mode
d. Mode

Refer to the following for questions 15–17:

The Prohibition era in the United States lasted from 1920 to 1933. It was a period in which the sale, production, and transport of alcohol was banned nationwide. The ban was enforced by the 18th Amendment to the Constitution, which stated:

"After one year from the ratification of this article the manufacture, sale, or transportation of intoxicating liquors within, the importation thereof into, or the exportation thereof from the United States and all territory subject to the jurisdiction thereof for beverage purposes is hereby prohibited."

During the Prohibition era, the crime rate increased by 24%. Organized crime increased, and criminal syndicates operated an illegal alcohol trade. Those participating in organized crime profited from bootlegging alcohol and transporting it to speakeasies, where people could still secretly access alcohol.

In 1933, the 21st Amendment was added to the Constitution. It states, "The eighteenth article of amendment to the Constitution of the United States is hereby repealed."

15. Which of the following pieces of information from the passage is an example of causation?

a. The crime rate increased by 24%, then criminals bootlegged alcohol.
b. The sale of alcohol was banned, then the use of liquors was prohibited.
c. Alcohol was prohibited, then organized crime increased.
d. People drank in speakeasies, then they secretly accessed alcohol.

16. Which of the following was a likely result of the passage of the 21st Amendment?

a. People protested.
b. Crime syndicates increased.
c. Speakeasies continued to operate.
d. The crime rate decreased.

17. What does the word *repealed* most closely mean in this passage?

a. Revoked
b. Extended
c. Enforced
d. Initiated

Refer to the following for questions 18–20:

The following excerpts are from Articles V and VI of the Articles of Confederation, which were adopted by the Continental Congress in 1777 and used as the first constitution of the United States from 1781 until they were replaced by the modern Constitution in 1789.

Article V. For the more convenient management of the general interests of the united states, delegates shall be annually appointed in such manner as the legislature of each state shall direct, to meet in Congress on the first Monday in November, in every year, with a power reserved to each state to recall its delegates, or any of them, at any time within the year, and to send others in their stead, for the remainder of the Year.

No State shall be represented in Congress by less than two, nor by more than seven Members; and no person shall be capable of being delegate for more than three years, in any term of six years; nor shall any person, being a delegate, be capable of holding any office under the united states, for which he, or another for his benefit receives any salary, fees or emolument of any kind.

Each State shall maintain its own delegates in a meeting of the states, and while they act as members of the committee of the states.

In determining questions in the united states, in Congress assembled, each state shall have one vote.

Freedom of speech and debate in Congress shall not be impeached or questioned in any Court, or place out of Congress, and the members of congress shall be protected in their persons from arrests and imprisonments, during the time of their going to and from, and attendance on congress, except for treason, felony, or breach of the peace.

Article VI (excerpt):

No vessels of war shall be kept up in time of peace, by any state, except such number only, as shall be deemed necessary by the united states, in congress assembled, for the defence of such state, or its trade; nor shall any body of forces be kept up, by any state, in time of peace, except such number only as, in the judgment of the united states, in congress assembled, shall be deemed requisite to garrison the forts necessary for the defence of such state; but every state shall always keep up a well regulated and disciplined militia, sufficiently armed and accoutred, and shall provide and constantly have ready for use, in public stores, a due number of field pieces and tents, and a proper quantity of arms, ammunition, and camp equipage.

18. Which of the following was a weakness of Article V?

a. Small states had a disproportionate amount of power in Congress.
b. Some delegates received compensation for their term in Congress.
c. Freedom of speech and debate could be stifled within Congress.
d. Not every state was able to send a delegate as a representative to Congress.

19. Which of the following issues could arise from Article VI?

a. Troops would not be ready to assemble unless a conflict arose.
b. States would need to always keep forts and vessels of war ready.
c. States could have a disproportionate number of military supplies.
d. The federal government could have a difficult time defending itself.

20. What does the word *recall* in Article V most closely mean?

a. Order to come back to Congress
b. Decide between two options
c. Remove a person from their position
d. Remember a previous fact

Refer to the following for questions 21–23:

The following is an excerpt of President Roosevelt's speech to Congress the day after Japan's attack on Pearl Harbor.

Yesterday, December 7, 1941—a date which will live in infamy—the United States of America was suddenly and deliberately attacked by naval and air forces of the Empire of Japan.

The United States was at peace with that Nation and, at the solicitation of Japan, was still in conversation with its Government and its Emperor looking toward the maintenance of peace in the Pacific. Indeed, one hour after Japanese air squadrons had commenced bombing in the American Island of Oahu, the Japanese Ambassador to the United States and his colleague delivered to our Secretary of State a formal reply to a recent American message. And while this reply stated that it seemed useless to continue the existing diplomatic negotiations, it contained no threat or hint of war or of armed attack.

It will be recorded that the distance of Hawaii from Japan makes it obvious that the attack was deliberately planned many days or even weeks ago. During the intervening time the Japanese Government has deliberately sought to deceive the United States by false statements and expressions of hope for continued peace.

The following is an excerpt of an announcement by the Japanese government to the people of Japan after the attack.

What an uproar! Japan's Imperial Forces got things off to a quick start with one splendid strike then another in historic surprise attacks on Pearl Harbor, where the bravado of the US Asia fleet met with sudden defeat, and off the Malaya Coast, where the main forces of the British Asia fleet were utterly annihilated. Word has it that Roosevelt and Churchill were shaken up and went pale upon hearing of the defeats. In a third strike, Hong Kong Island, England's strategic base for its 100-year exploitation of East Asia, fell into ruin in only a matter of ten days. During this time, Churchill was sent reeling, cutting off contact with others and showing up in Washington.

What these two headstrong countries are striving for will only lead them on a downhill path to military defeat. Our barbaric enemies are already cowering in fear in the Pacific, and the fall of Manila shall mark the day of the Philippines' subjugation and reversion back to Greater East Asia. The enemy power of Singapore, which was—alas—boasting of its impenetrable stronghold before the Imperial Forces penetrated the jungle area of the Malay Peninsula and advanced southward like a raging tide, shall also vanish into nothingness in the midst of this glorious chapter in history.

21. Which of the following is a similarity between Roosevelt's address and Japan's announcement?

a. They both characterized the Japanese military as victorious.
b. They both described the attack as a surprise.
c. They both explained the attack's effect on England.
d. They both portrayed the Philippines as allies.

22. Which of the following sentences or phrases from these excerpts does NOT contain any opinions?

a. "Japan's Imperial Forces got things off to a quick start with one splendid strike then another in historic surprise attacks on Pearl Harbor..."
b. "What these two headstrong countries are striving for will only lead them on a downhill path to military defeat."
c. "...one hour after Japanese air squadrons had commenced bombing in the American Island of Oahu, the Japanese Ambassador to the United States and his colleague delivered to our Secretary of State a formal reply to a recent American message."
d. The enemy power of Singapore, which was—alas—boasting of its impenetrable stronghold before the Imperial Forces penetrated the jungle area of the Malay Peninsula and advanced southward like a raging tide, shall also vanish into nothingness in the midst of this glorious chapter in history.

23. How did these two excerpts portray the same event differently?

a. The president's address described the attack as an event of ongoing conflict, while the announcement to Japan described the attack as unforeseen.
b. The president's address described the attack as a minor event, while the announcement to Japan described the attack as a historic event.
c. The president's address described the attack as an accident, while the announcement to Japan described the attack as deliberate.
d. The president's address described the attack as a threat that will lead to conflict, while the announcement to Japan described the attack as leading to a decisive victory.

Refer to the following for questions 24–25:

An economist is researching the causes of recent inflation in the US. She decides to look at the unemployment rate as a potential factor.

Year	Employment (%)	Inflation (%)
1981	59	4
1982	57.8	3.8
1983	57.9	3.9
1984	59.5	3.9
1985	60.1	4
1986	60.7	4.4
1987	61.5	4.4
1988	62.3	4.6
1989	63	6.1
1990	62.8	3.1
1991	61.7	2.9
1992	61.5	2.7

24. Which of the following best characterizes the relationship between the inflation rate and the unemployment rate in this chart?

a. Positive correlation
b. Inverse correlation
c. Absolute correlation
d. Non-linear correlation

25. Which of the following describes why the unemployment rate is an independent variable in this research?

a. The unemployment rate is unrelated to the inflation rate.
b. The unemployment rate is what the economist is trying to find the cause of.
c. The unemployment rate is potentially causing the changes in the inflation rate.
d. The unemployment rate is impacted by changes in the inflation rate.

Refer to the following for question 26:

This chart illustrates the population of Washington, DC by race from 1810 to 2010.

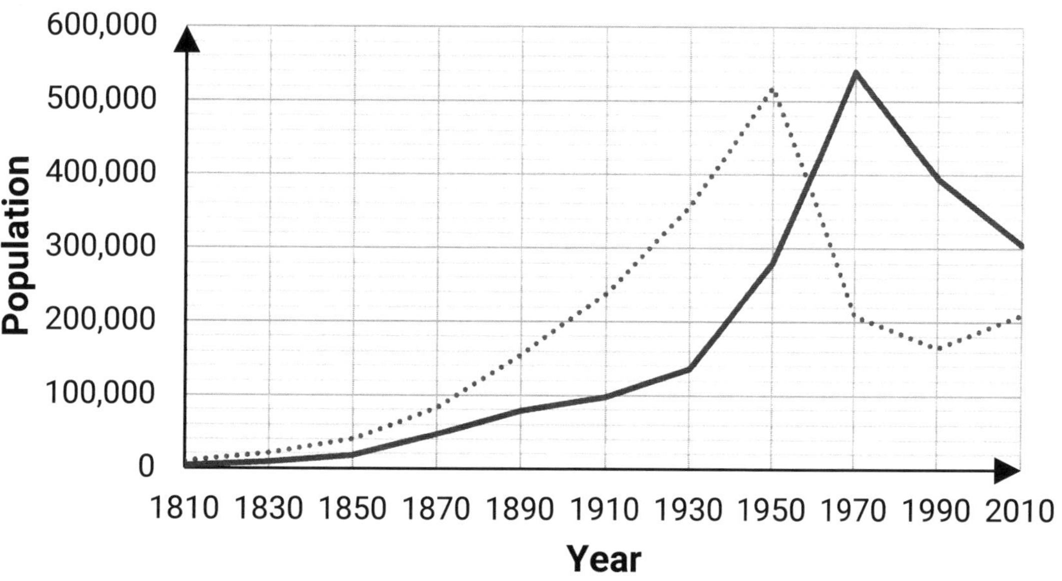

Washington, DC was founded in 1790. Its population grew slowly for the first 70 years. In 1800, Washington, DC became the capital of the United States. In 1860, most of the population of the city was white. At the start of the Civil War, the population increased significantly. The population continued to increase after World War I and World War II. After the wars, many white Americans began an exodus to the suburbs. After Martin Luther King Jr. was assassinated, black Americans also began leaving for the suburbs.

26. During which of the following years did black Americans begin to leave the city?

a. 1950
b. 1970
c. 1990
d. 2000

Refer to the following for questions 27–29:

The following is an excerpt from a Time magazine article titled "Nation: A War at War," which ran on May 18, 1970. At this time, the Nixon administration was reducing the number of troops in Vietnam while relying more heavily on South Vietnam's military. Two weeks earlier, on May 4, thirteen unarmed students at Kent State University had been shot by the Ohio National Guard during an anti-war protest. Four died.

Both the eruption of protest and the reaction to it mocked Nixon's still unfulfilled promise to lead the nation "forward together." Not only were there rending, sometimes bloody clashes between peace demonstrators and peace officers, but a scattering of vicious brawls set citizen against citizen as well.

Not long ago, the Administration was considered an artful, managerial mechanism, oiled with serenity, unanimity and self-confidence. Now it showed symptoms of severe internal distress. Interior Secretary Walter Hickel's letter of criticism to the President (see box, page 10) and the abrupt resignation of two young Administration staffers were among the most tangible signs of strain. There were also hints of basic disagreement in the Cabinet over the Cambodian decision—hints that Nixon declined to deny at a hastily called press conference. On Capitol Hill dissension increased daily.

The President had carefully calculated the diplomatic and military hazards of invading the Cambodian sanctuaries. But the more important risk involved the response at home—and in that crucial area he has proved to be dangerously wrong. Nixon, to be sure, could not have foreseen the Kent State shootings.

But he was sadly slow in recognizing their impact. After the four students were gunned down, he found no reason to censure the Guardsmen. All he could bring himself to say was: "When dissent turns to violence, it invites tragedy." That much was obvious. It seemed equally clear that even if the Cambodian expedition should accomplish more than now appears likely, it has already destroyed far more American resources of morale and cohesion than any North Vietnamese supplies could be worth.

27. Which of the following best characterizes how the evolving situation of the Vietnam War shaped this author's point of view?

a. The president's decision to invade Cambodia increased public support of the war and gave the author a favorable view of the war effort.
b. Nixon's response to the lack of support at home regarding the war created a decline in morale and gave the author an unfavorable view of the war effort.
c. Nixon's reaction to the Kent State shootings bolstered morale at home and gave the author a favorable view of the war effort.
d. The public's positive reactions toward Nixon's policies regarding the war encouraged the president to show more confidence and gave the author an unfavorable view of the war effort.

28. Which of the following is an example of the author using a solely factual statement?

a. "But he was sadly slow in recognizing their impact."
b. "...the Administration was considered an artful, managerial mechanism..."
c. "...four students were gunned down..."
d. "...in that crucial area he has proved to be dangerously wrong."

29. Which of the following statements shows the author's bias?

a. "The President had carefully calculated the diplomatic and military hazards of invading the Cambodian sanctuaries."
b. "...he found no reason to censure the Guardsmen."
c. "There were also hints of basic disagreement in the Cabinet over the Cambodian decision."
d. "...the eruption of protest and the reaction to it mocked Nixon's still unfulfilled promise to lead the nation 'forward together.'"

Refer to the following for questions 30–32:

For a bill to become law, the bill must first be introduced by a member of the Senate or the House of Representatives. The bill can be related to a wide range of issues, including policies or budget considerations. The bill is then assigned a code that depends on where it originated. After the bill is assigned a code, it is referred to the relevant focused committee in that house of Congress based on the type of issue it involves. The focused committee analyzes the bill and gathers input and testimony from experts on the topic. The committee can amend, rewrite, or reject the bill before it gets any further. If a majority of the committee members approve of the bill, it moves to the full chamber.

Once the bill is introduced to the full chamber, it is discussed and debated. Amendments can be proposed. Once the debate has ended, the chamber votes on the bill. If the majority of the chamber is in favor, the bill will advance. When a bill is approved by either the Senate or House of Representatives, it then goes to the other house for debate and approval. If either house fails to pass the bill, it will die. If the bill is passed by both houses of Congress, it goes forward to the final phase, in which the president acts on the bill.

Once the bill reaches the president, it becomes law either if he immediately signs it or if he lets it sit 10 days without signing it. If Congress adjourns before 10 days have passed, and the president has not signed the bill yet, it will not become law. This cannot be overridden. The president also has the option of vetoing the bill. If this happens, the bill will be sent back to Congress. Congress can either revise the bill and try to get it passed again, or they can override the president's veto with two-thirds of their votes in favor of the bill in both houses.

30. Suppose a bill called H.R.4365 is introduced. What are the next three steps that the bill could follow?

a. The bill is referred to a committee in the House of Representatives. The committee analyzes the bill and then revises it prior to the next step.
b. The bill is voted upon by the Senate. Then, it is approved by the House of Representatives and sent to the president to act upon.
c. The bill is referred to a committee in the Senate. It is voted upon by the full chamber and then debated in the House of Representatives.
d. The bill is debated in the House of Representatives. If the House of Representatives approves of the bill, it is then sent to the Senate for approval.

31. Which of the following is an example of the checks and balances built into the process?

a. The committee analyzes bills, and then they can approve them.
b. The bill is introduced by a member of the Senate or House of Representatives, and it is assigned a code.
c. The Senate and House of Representatives create bills, and the president can veto them.
d. A bill is introduced within the full chamber, and it is debated and discussed.

32. What does the word *override* most closely mean in this passage?

a. To advance a bill through Congress
b. To approve a decision by majority vote
c. To send a bill for further consideration
d. To use authority to cancel or reject a decision

Refer to the following for question 33:

The following speech is one in a series of four-minute speeches organized by the Committee of Public Information in 1917 during World War I.

"Ladies and Gentlemen, I have just received the information that there is a German spy among us—a German spy watching us.

He is around, here somewhere, reporting upon you and me—sending reports about us to Berlin and telling the Germans just what we are doing with the Liberty Loan.

From every section of the country these spies have been getting reports over to Potsdam—not general reports but details—where the loan is going well and where its success seems weak, and what people are saying in each community.

For the German government is worried about our great loan. Those Junkers fear its effect upon the German morale. They're raising a loan this month, too.

If the American people lend their billions now, one and all with a hip-hip-hurrah, it means that America is united and strong. While, if we lend our money half-heartedly, America seems weak and autocracy remains strong.

Money means everything now; it means a quicker victory and therefore less bloodshed. We are in the war, and now Americans can have but one opinion, only one wish in the Liberty Loan.

Well, I hope these spies are getting their messages straight, letting Potsdam know that America is hurling back to the autocrats these answers:

For treachery here, attempted treachery in Mexico, treachery everywhere—one billion.

For murder of American women and children—one billion more.

For broken faith and promise to murder more Americans—billions and billions more.

And then we will add:

In the world fight for Liberty, our share—billions and billions and billions and endless billions.

Do not let the German spy hear and report that you are a slacker."

33. Which of the following best describes the purpose of this speech?

a. It is an entreaty to help the speaker find the spy in their presence.
b. It is propaganda meant to raise money for the war.
c. It is a warning to beware of the actions of Germany.
d. It is an appeal to assist with raising German morale.

Refer to the following for question 34:

The following is an excerpt from a speech from President Franklin D. Roosevelt, which he delivered 11 months before the attack on Pearl Harbor.

"In the future days, which we seek to make secure, we look forward to a world founded upon four essential human freedoms.

The first is freedom of speech and expression—everywhere in the world.

The second is freedom of every person to worship God in his own way—everywhere in the world.

The third is freedom from want—which, translated into world terms, means economic understandings which will secure to every nation a healthy peacetime life for its inhabitants—everywhere in the world.

The fourth is freedom from fear—which, translated into world terms, means a world-wide reduction of armaments to such a point and in such a thorough fashion that no nation will be in a position to commit an act of physical aggression against any neighbor—anywhere in the world.

That is no vision of a distant millennium. It is a definite basis for a kind of world attainable in our own time and generation. That kind of world is the very antithesis of the so-called new order of tyranny which the dictators seek to create with the crash of a bomb.

To that new order we oppose the greater conception—the moral order. A good society is able to face schemes of world domination and foreign revolutions alike without fear.

Since the beginning of our American history, we have been engaged in change—in a perpetual peaceful revolution—a revolution which goes on steadily, quietly adjusting itself to changing conditions—without the concentration camp or the quick-lime in the ditch. The world order which we seek is the cooperation of free countries, working together in a friendly, civilized society.

This nation has placed its destiny in the hands and heads and hearts of its millions of free men and women, and its faith in freedom under the guidance of God. Freedom means the supremacy of human rights everywhere. Our support goes to those who struggle to gain those rights or keep them. Our strength is our unity of purpose. To that high concept there can be no end save victory."

34. Which of the following best describes how this speech could relate to the US' entry into World War II, which was precipitated by Japan's attack on Pearl Harbor?

a. This speech could deter Americans from participating in war out of fear of losing their freedoms.
b. This speech could convince Americans that war is not in their best interest.
c. The speech could be used as justification for the US to enter into war.
d. This speech could forewarn Americans against letting other countries gain these freedoms.

Refer to the following for question 35:

This chart shows the number of internet users per 100 people and GDP per capita, as of 2017. Economists believe that widespread internet use in any country has a strong positive effect on the country's economic growth. Internet usage drives business growth, job creation, and economic modernization. The chart shows that countries with a higher percentage of internet users also have a higher GDP per capita.

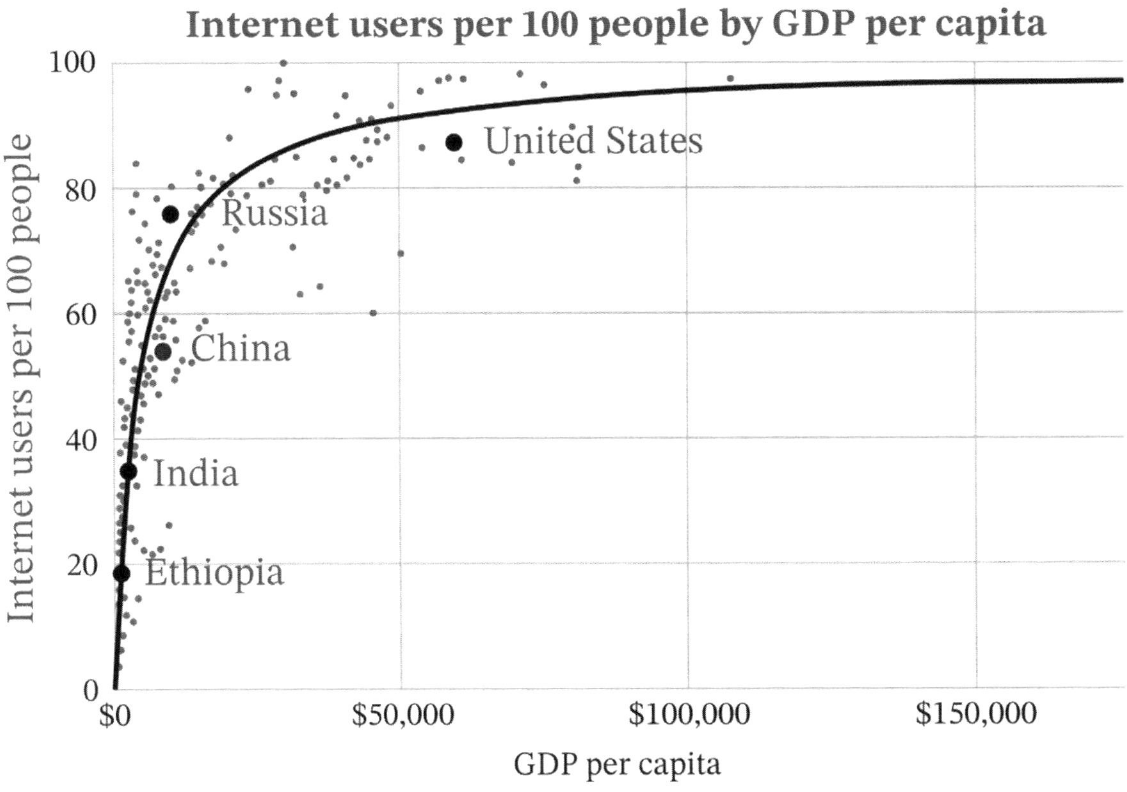

35. According to the chart, what level of internet usage has the strongest effect on GDP?

a. 40-60%
b. 10-30%
c. 70-90%
d. 0-10%

Refer to the following for questions 36–38:

Article II Section 1 of the Constitution of the United States:

The executive Power shall be vested in a President of the United States of America.

He shall hold his Office during the Term of four Years, and, together with the Vice President, chosen for the same Term, be elected, as follows:

Each State shall appoint, in such Manner as the Legislature thereof may direct, a Number of Electors, equal to the whole Number of Senators and Representatives to which the State may be entitled in the Congress: but no Senator or Representative, or Person holding an Office of Trust or Profit under the United States, shall be appointed an Elector.

...

In Case of the Removal of the President from Office, or of his Death, Resignation, or Inability to discharge the Powers and Duties of the said Office, the Same shall devolve on the Vice President, and the Congress may by Law provide for the Case of Removal, Death, Resignation or Inability, both of the President and Vice President, declaring what Officer shall then act as President, and such Officer shall act accordingly, until the Disability be removed, or a President shall be elected.

The President shall, at stated Times, receive for his Services, a Compensation, which shall neither be increased nor diminished during the Period for which he shall have been elected, and he shall not receive within that Period any other Emolument from the United States, or any of them.

25th Amendment to the Constitution:

Section 1

In case of the removal of the President from office or of his death or resignation, the Vice President shall become President.

Section 2

Whenever there is a vacancy in the office of the Vice President, the President shall nominate a Vice President who shall take office upon confirmation by a majority vote of both Houses of Congress.

Section 3

Whenever the President transmits to the President pro tempore of the Senate and the Speaker of the House of Representatives his written declaration that he is unable to discharge the powers and duties of his office, and until he transmits to them a written declaration to the contrary, such powers and duties shall be discharged by the Vice President as Acting President.

36. Which part of Article II of the Constitution does Section 1 of the 25th Amendment reiterate?

a. "The executive Power shall be vested in a President of the United States of America."
b. "...the Congress may by Law provide for the Case of Removal, Death, Resignation or Inability, both of the President and Vice President, declaring what Officer shall then act as President..."
c. "In Case of the Removal of the President from Office, or of his Death, Resignation, or Inability to discharge the Powers and Duties of the said Office, the Same shall devolve on the Vice President..."
d. "no Senator or Representative, or Person holding an Office of Trust or Profit under the United States, shall be appointed an Elector..."

37. Which of the following does the word *emolument*, as used in Article II, most closely mean?

a. Classified information from the government
b. Appointment of a new person to office
c. The powers given to the elected president
d. A payment or fee from serving in office

38. Which of the following is the main purpose of Sections 1 and 2 of the 25th Amendment?

a. It establishes the next steps if a president or vice president cannot or will not perform his or her duties any longer.
b. It describes Congress's responsibilities in choosing a replacement for the vice president.
c. It confirms that while the president might leave office due to death, he or she cannot resign.
d. It relays the steps that the vice president might take to choose his or her own replacement.

Refer to the following for questions 39–41:

During the American Civil War, President Abraham Lincoln issued a presidential statement called the Preliminary Emancipation Proclamation on September 22, 1862. Exactly 100 days later, on January 1, 1863, he issued the Emancipation Proclamation, which enacted the laws described in the Preliminary Emancipation Proclamation.

Excerpt from the Preliminary Emancipation Proclamation:

I, Abraham Lincoln, President of the United States of America, and Commander-in-Chief of the Army and Navy thereof, do hereby proclaim and declare that hereafter, as heretofore, the war will be prosecuted for the object of practically restoring the constitutional relation between the United States, and each of the States, and the people thereof, in which States that relation is, or may be, suspended or disturbed.

...

That on the first day of January in the year of our Lord, one thousand eight hundred and sixty-three, all persons held as slaves within any State, or designated part of a State, the people whereof shall then be in rebellion against the United States shall be then, thenceforward, and forever free; and the executive government of the United States, including the military and naval authority thereof, will recognize and maintain the freedom of such persons, and will do no act or acts to repress such persons, or any of them, in any efforts they may make for their actual freedom.

That the executive will, on the first day of January aforesaid, by proclamation, designate the States, and part of States, if any, in which the people thereof respectively, shall then be in rebellion against the United States; and the fact that any State, or the people thereof shall, on that day be, in good faith represented in the Congress of the United States, by members chosen thereto, at elections wherein a majority of the qualified voters of such State shall have participated, shall, in the absence of strong countervailing testimony, be deemed conclusive evidence that such State and the people thereof, are not then in rebellion against the United States.

39. Which of the following was the main consequence of the Preliminary Emancipation Proclamation?

a. The prosecution of individuals who gave aid to slave states
b. The continuation of the war to suppress the current rebellion
c. An order to free the slaves within states that were part of the rebellion
d. A discontinuation of the practice of slavery during the war

40. Which of the following is a way in which the Emancipation Proclamation may have contributed to ending the war?

a. It supported the prosecution of the rebelling army.
b. It gave slaves the right to vote.
c. It forced slaves to join the military forces.
d. It removed resources from the rebelling states.

41. Which of the following might be a reason that President Lincoln made the Preliminary Emancipation Proclamation go into effect in 100 days rather than immediately?

a. To encourage slaves to work harder to help rebelling states
b. To give states time to end their rebellion and keep slavery
c. To force the military and naval authorities to support the proclamation
d. To allow slaves the ability to leave rebelling states on their own

Refer to the following for question 42:

On December 8, 1963, President Dwight D. Eisenhower gave a speech to the UN General Assembly called "Atoms for Peace." This speech took place after the US had already used nuclear weapons, and the Soviet Union had its own nuclear capability. The following is an excerpt from that speech.

I know that the American people share my deep belief that if a danger exists in the world, it is a danger shared by all; and equally, that if hope exists in the mind of one nation, that hope should be shared by all. Finally, if there is to be advanced any proposal designed to ease even by the smallest measure the tensions of today's world, what more appropriate audience could there be than the members of the General Assembly of the United Nations.

I feel impelled to speak today in a language that in a sense is new, one which I, who have spent so much of my life in the military profession, would have preferred never to use. That new language is the language of atomic warfare.

The atomic age has moved forward at such a pace that every citizen of the world should have some comprehension, at least in comparative terms, of the extent of this development, of the utmost significance to every one of us. Clearly, if the peoples of the world are to conduct an intelligent search for peace, they must be armed with the significant facts of today's existence.

My recital of atomic danger and power is necessarily stated in United States terms, for these are the only incontrovertible facts that I know, I need hardly point out to this Assembly, however, that this subject is global, not merely national in character.

On 16 July 1945, the United States set off the world's biggest atomic explosion. Since that date in 1945, the United States of America has conducted forty-two test explosions. Atomic bombs are more than twenty-five times as powerful as the weapons with which the atomic age dawned, while hydrogen weapons are in the ranges of millions of tons of TNT equivalent.

...

I would be prepared to submit to the Congress of the United States, and with every expectation of approval, any such plan that would, first, encourage world-wide investigation into the most effective peacetime uses of fissionable material, and with the certainty that the investigators had all the material needed for the conducting of all experiments that were appropriate; second, begin to diminish the potential destructive power of the world's atomic stockpiles; third, allow all peoples of all nations to see that, in this enlightened age, the great Powers of the earth, both of the East and of the West, are interested in human aspirations first rather than in building up the armaments of war; fourth, open up a new channel for peaceful discussion and initiative at least a new approach to the many difficult problems that must be solved in both private and public conversations if the world is to shake off the inertia imposed by fear and is to make positive progress towards peace.

Against the dark background of the atomic bomb, the United States does not wish merely to present strength, but also the desire and the hope for peace. The coming months will be fraught with fateful decisions. In this Assembly, in the capitals and military headquarters of the world, in the hearts of men everywhere, be they governed or governors, may they be the decisions which will lead this world out of fear and into peace.

42. Which of the following best describes how historical context shaped Eisenhower's point of view in his speech?

a. The nuclear arms race had begun recently, so Eisenhower acknowledged the potential fear associated with nuclear weapons and then assured the UN General Assembly that the US could still work toward peace.
b. The US had not yet used nuclear weapons, so Eisenhower implored the General Assembly to allow it to adopt the use of atomic bombs and use them to its advantage.
c. Eisenhower was unaware of any danger associated with the use of atomic weapons, so he asked the US to begin researching all possible uses of fissionable material.
d. The General Assembly had not yet heard of the danger of atomic weapons, so Eisenhower described the pros and cons of nuclear weapons while insisting that the US should discontinue using them.

Refer to the following for question 43:

The following was written as an opinion on campaign finance reform:

> "When candidates run for office, they raise money to fund their campaigns. These funds are used for advertising, travel, staff salaries, supplies, equipment, and more fundraising. When a candidate receives donations, he or she can spend the money to gain familiarity with voters, and since voters are more likely to vote for people with recognizable names, the candidate can also gain popularity among voters. Campaign finance laws currently dictate how much and in what ways a candidate can receive from individuals, political action committees (PACs), and political party committees. Despite these laws, the amount of money raised and spent by candidates is often disparate, with a few candidates gaining a major advantage with their large sum of campaign funds. To even out the playing field, campaign funding should be limited to small donors, and a cap should be placed on how much a campaign can spend. Even better, each candidate should be provided with a set amount to spend on their campaign, and no more."

The chart shows the 2004 candidates for president, as well as their total spending on campaigns. Bush and Kerry became the Republican and Democratic nominees, respectively.

Candidate	Total Spending	% of Popular Vote
George W. Bush	$367,228,819	50.73%
John Kerry	$328,479,256	48.27%
Ralph Nader	$4,572,638	0.38%
Michael Badnarik	$1,093,018	0.32%
Michael Peroutka	$709,091	0.12%
David Cobb	$493,727	0.10%

43. Which of the following best describes whether the mean is a good measure of central tendency for the candidates' total spending?

a. It is, because it accurately represents spending for a typical candidate.
b. It is, because it shows the amount that most campaigns spend.
c. It is not, because the mean is skewed by the significantly higher numbers from the candidates with the highest spending.
d. It is not, because it only shows the difference between the highest and lowest amounts of spending.

Refer to the following for question 44:

This poster was used in the United States during World War I.

44. Which of the following best describes the purpose of this poster?

a. It was a warning for more people to stay home from the war.
b. It was an entreaty for eligible people to join the military.
c. It was an invitation for people to interview to work at Third Liberty Loan.
d. It was propaganda encouraging people to fund the war through the Third Liberty Loan program.

Refer to the following for question 45:

On April 16, 1963, Martin Luther King Jr. wrote an open letter from Birmingham Jail. King had been arrested during the Birmingham Campaign, which was a series of coordinated sit-ins and marches against racial segregation and racism in Birmingham, AL. This is an excerpt from that letter.

> Now, what is the difference between the two? How does one determine whether a law is just or unjust? A just law is a man made code that squares with the moral law or the law of God. An unjust law is a code that is out of harmony with the moral law. To put it in the terms of St. Thomas Aquinas: An unjust law is a human law that is not rooted in eternal law and natural law. Any law that uplifts human personality is just. Any law that degrades human personality is unjust. All segregation statutes are unjust because segregation distorts the soul and damages the personality. It gives the segregator a false sense of superiority and the segregated a false sense of inferiority. Segregation, to use the terminology of the Jewish philosopher Martin Buber, substitutes an "I it" relationship for an "I thou" relationship and ends up

relegating persons to the status of things. Hence segregation is not only politically, economically and sociologically unsound, it is morally wrong and sinful. Paul Tillich has said that sin is separation. Is not segregation an existential expression of man's tragic separation, his awful estrangement, his terrible sinfulness? Thus it is that I can urge men to obey the 1954 decision of the Supreme Court, for it is morally right; and I can urge them to disobey segregation ordinances, for they are morally wrong.

Let us consider a more concrete example of just and unjust laws. An unjust law is a code that a numerical or power majority group compels a minority group to obey but does not make binding on itself. This is difference made legal. By the same token, a just law is a code that a majority compels a minority to follow and that it is willing to follow itself. This is sameness made legal. Let me give another explanation. A law is unjust if it is inflicted on a minority that, as a result of being denied the right to vote, had no part in enacting or devising the law. Who can say that the legislature of Alabama which set up that state's segregation laws was democratically elected? Throughout Alabama all sorts of devious methods are used to prevent Negroes from becoming registered voters, and there are some counties in which, even though Negroes constitute a majority of the population, not a single Negro is registered. Can any law enacted under such circumstances be considered democratically structured?

Sometimes a law is just on its face and unjust in its application. For instance, I have been arrested on a charge of parading without a permit. Now, there is nothing wrong in having an ordinance which requires a permit for a parade. But such an ordinance becomes unjust when it is used to maintain segregation and to deny citizens the First-Amendment privilege of peaceful assembly and protest.

I hope you are able to see the distinction I am trying to point out. In no sense do I advocate evading or defying the law, as would the rabid segregationist. That would lead to anarchy. One who breaks an unjust law must do so openly, lovingly, and with a willingness to accept the penalty. I submit that an individual who breaks a law that conscience tells him is unjust, and who willingly accepts the penalty of imprisonment in order to arouse the conscience of the community over its injustice, is in reality expressing the highest respect for law.

45. Which of the following lines from this letter is solely a fact?

a. "Throughout Alabama all sorts of devious methods are used to prevent Negroes from becoming registered voters..."
b. "For instance, I have been arrested on a charge of parading without a permit."
c. "All segregation statutes are unjust because segregation distorts the soul and damages the personality."
d. "One who breaks an unjust law must do so openly, lovingly, and with a willingness to accept the penalty."

Refer to the following for questions 46–47:

This chart shows the annual inflation rate and the nominal interest rate in the US by year. The inflation rate shows how much the cost of goods and services has gone up over one year. The nominal interest rate is the interest rate set by the Federal Reserve. This rate is used as a benchmark for financial transactions throughout the country.

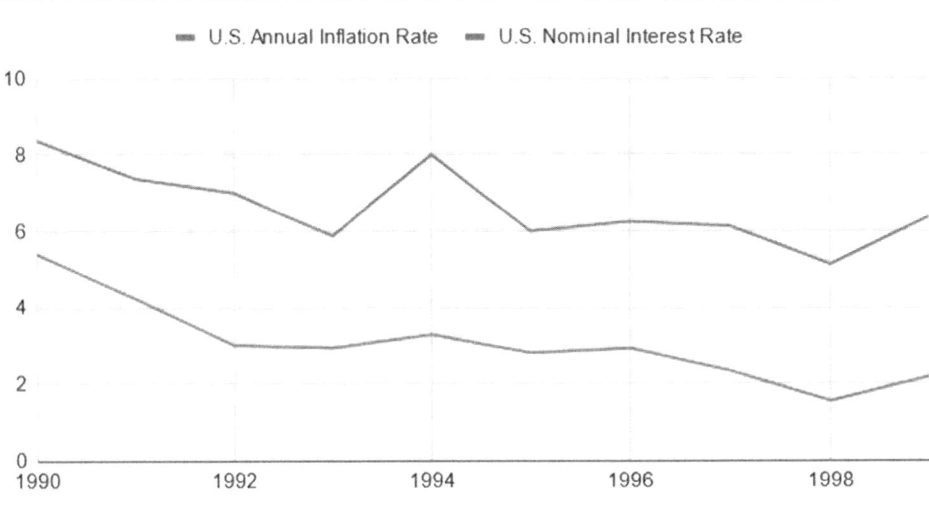

46. Which of the following best characterizes the relationship between the US annual inflation rate and the US nominal interest rate?

a. Positive correlation
b. Absolute correlation
c. Inverse correlation
d. Negative correlation

47. Which of the following could explain the relationship between the US annual inflation rate and the US nominal interest rate?

a. When the nominal interest rate is high, the Federal Reserve tries to lower the cost of making financial transactions.
b. When inflation is low, banks and lenders gain more money from financial transactions, so the nominal interest rate is higher.
c. When the nominal interest rate is low, people spend less on financial transactions, which raises inflation.
d. When inflation is high, the Federal Reserve wants to reduce borrowing and spending to attempt to control inflation.

Refer to the following for questions 48–51:

The Lewis and Clark Expedition began in Camp Wood, IL in May 1804. The expedition was led by Meriwether Lewis and William Clark. Joseph Whitehouse was a private in the expedition and also served as the group's tailor. The following accounts are from March 23, 1806.

William Clark:

This morning proved So raney and uncertain that we were undeturmined for Some time whether we had best Set out & risque the [river?] which appeared to be riseing or not. Jo. Colter returned haveing killed an Elk about 3 miles towards Point

Adams. the rained Seased and it became fair about Meridean, at which time we loaded our Canoes & at 1 P. M. left Fort Clatsop on our homeward bound journey. at this place we had wintered and remained from the 7th of Decr. 1805 to this day and have lived as well as we had any right to expect, and we can Say that we were never one day without 3 meals of Some kind a day either pore Elk meat or roots, not withstanding the repeeted fall of rain which has fallen almost Constantly Since we passed the long narrows on the [blank] of Novr. last indeed w[e] have had only [blank] days fair weather since that time. Soon after we had Set out from Fort Clatsop we were met by De lash el wilt & 8 men of the Chinnooks, and Delashelwilts wife the old boud and his Six Girls, they had, a Canoe, a Sea otter Skin, Dried fish and hats for Sale, we purchased a Sea otter Skin, and proceeded on, thro' Meriwethers Bay, there was a Stiff breese from the S. W. which raised Considerable Swells around Meriwethers point which was as much as our Canoes Could ride. above point William we came too at the Camp of Drewyer & the 2 Field's. they had killed 2 Elk which was about 1½ miles distant. here we Encampd. for the night having made 16 miles.

Joseph Whitehouse:

Sunday March 23d At 1 o'Clock P. M. we embarked, on board our Canoes from Fort Clatsop, on our homeward bound Voyage. We proceeded on up the South side of the Columbia River, when we were met by a party of the Chin-ook tribe of Indians, who belong to the Flatt head nation. These Indians were in Canoes, & were on their way to Fort Clatsop in Order to trade with us; they had with them a Canoe & a Sea Otter Skin, which they Intended trading with us. We halted a short time, & Captain Lewis purchased the Sea Otter skin from them. We then continued on our Voyage, and went round a point of land called by our officers Merryweather point (the Sirname of Captain Lewis) when the wind rose & blew hard from the South West, & the waves ran very high. We proceeded on, & passed another point of land called point William by our officers the Sirname of Captain Clark. We halted a short distance above this last point, at a Camp where the two hunters that were sent on ahead of us were. These two hunters had killed 2 Elk, which they informed us lay 1½ Miles from this place. We encamped at that place having come 16 Miles this day.

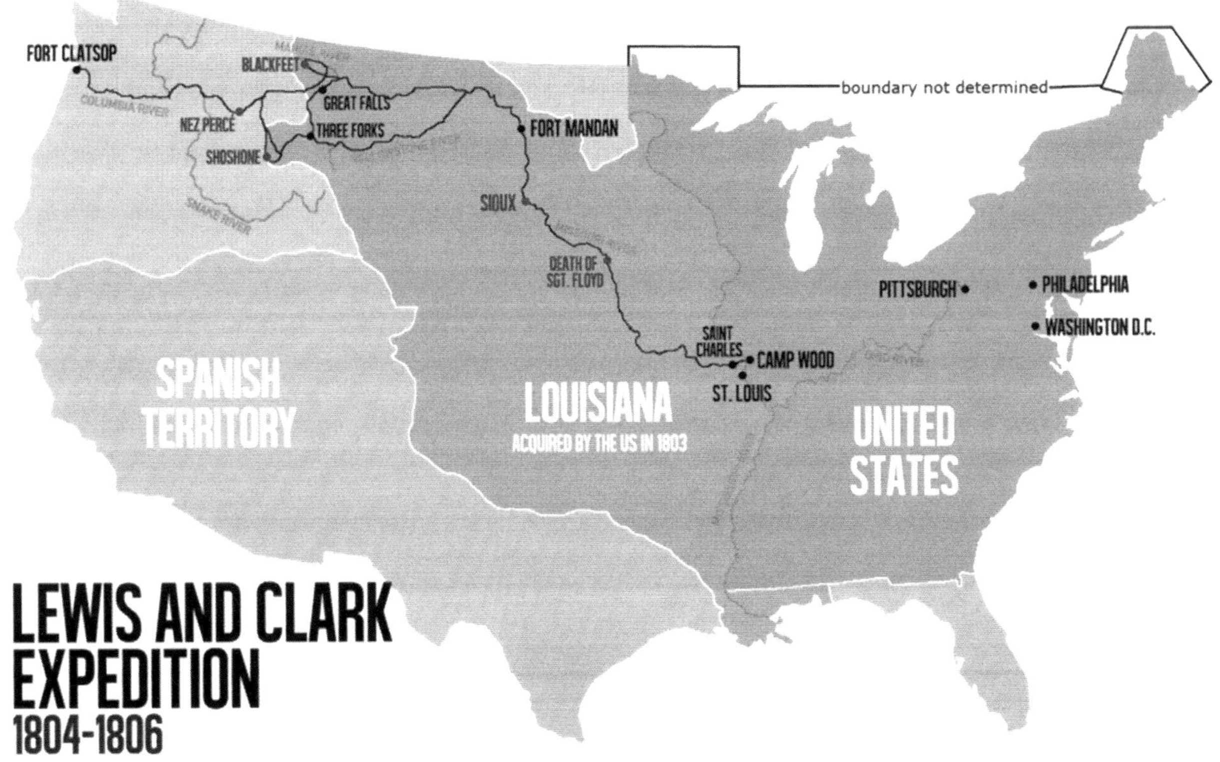

48. According to these accounts, which location on the map will be the next stop in their journey?

a. Sioux
b. St. Louis
c. Great Falls
d. Nez Perce

49. Which of the following describes how an author's account of events was shaped by his point of view?

a. Whitehouse served as a tailor, so he was looking forward to getting fabrics in trade from the Native Americans.
b. Clark was a leader of the expedition, so he was concerned about the safety of his team leaving that morning.
c. Because Whitehouse was mainly documenting their encounters with Native American tribes, he left out any mention of distances.
d. Clark was in charge of the food supplies for the expedition, so he documented the details of additions to their supply.

50. Which of the following best indicates whether Clark documented a reliable account of the day?

a. The similarities with Whitehouse's account of the day
b. The explanation that it will be their homeward journey
c. The use of Meriwether's name for landmarks
d. The omission of any mention of the rest of the crew on the journey

51. Which of the following was a result of the Lewis and Clark Expedition that benefited the United States?

a. The discovery of elk as food
b. The ability to travel in inclement weather
c. Geographic knowledge of the Spanish Territory
d. Trade and diplomacy with Native Americans

Refer to the following for question 52:

In February 1942, President Franklin D. Roosevelt issued Executive Order 9066 that called for the internment of Japanese Americans. This occurred in response to Japan's attack on Pearl Harbor and a growing fear about national security. The following excerpts are a letter from a Japanese American within one of the camps, writing to a teacher he knew, and a newspaper article about the internment.

Excerpt from the letter from Tetsuzo to Miss Breed, November 16, 1942:

> The food has been all right except for quantity...The medical situation here is pitiful. For that matter in all three camps. The main and the only hospital is at Camp I 15 miles away. Here in Camp III there is one young doctor with not too much experience and one student doctor working in an emergency clinic. They are supposed to take care of approximately 5000 people!!!! and they (the Big shots) wonder why we squawk about inadequate medical attention.
>
> No I haven't hiked to the river yet. I'd better do it soon cause there is going to be a fence around this camp!!!!!! 5 strands of barbed wire!!!!!!!!!! They say it's to keep the people out. . . . It's also to keep out cattle. Where in the cattle countries do they use 5 strands of barbed wire??

Excerpt of newspaper article from the San Francisco Chronicle, *May 21, 1942*:

> Three weeks ago this was empty land between two mountain ranges.
>
> Today it is a city of 3303 population with a fire department, a hospital, a police force, an English-language newspaper, baseball teams and community recreation centers.
>
> It probably is the fastest growing town in the world because soon its population will be doubled and eventually quadrupled.
>
> Most of the inhabitants are Japanese who have tasted American democracy and found it good. Probably 95 per cent at least of the Japanese here are loyal to the United States. They are the ones like S. Akamatsu, who moved into Building No. 6 and immediately put up pictures of George Washington, Abraham Lincoln and President Roosevelt.
>
> Many of the loyal ones came here with fear and doubt in their hearts, expecting a Nazi-type concentration camp. Instead they found comfortable wooden buildings covered with tar paper, bathhouses and showers and plenty of wholesome food.
>
> ...

Democracy is at work among them. An election has been held to choose block leaders. Eventually from these block leaders will be chosen an advisory committee of five to work with the camp management in preserving order and arranging for the planting of crops. Manzanar hopes to become a self-sufficient community when irrigation is brought to the rich but arid land.

The lives of the inhabitants have fallen quickly into the normal pattern of living. The Japanese firemen play solitaire while waiting for an alarm. A baby has been born and named Kenji Ogawa. Howard Kumagai, a mechanical engineer, has fallen in love with Kimiki Wakamura, former beauty shop operator, has proposed and been accepted. Boys and girls make dates for dances and for the movies where James Cagney is extremely popular.

52. How does each author's point of view lead to their description of the situation?

a. The author of the newspaper article gave an unbiased assessment of the internment since they experienced the situation, while Tetsuzo, who was interned, expressed only his fond memories of the camp.
b. As someone who was interned, Tetsuzo highlighted the poor conditions he experienced in the camp, while the author of the newspaper article, who was not directly impacted, praised the living conditions as comfortable.
c. The author of the newspaper article, who had family members in the camp, expressed outrage at the conditions they lived in, while Tetsuzo, who was in the camp himself, described the living conditions as comfortable.
d. Tetsuzo, who only received information through letters, described the deplorable conditions of the camp, while the author of the newspaper article, who visited the camp, included favorable descriptions.

Refer to the following for question 53:

On March 15, 1965, President Lyndon B. Johnson made a speech after a deadly violent incident in Selma, AL. Dr. Martin Luther King Jr. had planned a march to protest voting rights discrimination, and black Americans were attacked by police. After this speech, the Voting Rights Act of 1965 was introduced in Congress on March 17th, and the act was signed into law on August 6th. The act was intended to enforce those voting rights that were protected by the Fourteenth and Fifteenth Amendments. The following is an excerpt from Johnson's speech.

"This bill will establish a simple, uniform standard which cannot be used, however ingenious the effort, to flout our Constitution. It will provide for citizens to be registered by officials of the United States Government, if the state officials refuse to register them. It will eliminate tedious, unnecessary lawsuits which delay the right to vote. Finally, this legislation will ensure that properly registered individuals are not prohibited from voting. I will welcome the suggestions from all the members of Congress—I have no doubt that I will get some—on ways and means to strengthen this law and to make it effective.

But experience has plainly shown that this is the only path to carry out the command of the Constitution. To those who seek to avoid action by their national government in their home communities, who want to and who seek to maintain purely local control over elections, the answer is simple: open your polling places to all your people. Allow men and women to register and vote whatever the color of their skin. Extend the rights of citizenship to every citizen of this land. There is no

Constitutional issue here. The command of the Constitution is plain. There is no moral issue. It is wrong—deadly wrong—to deny any of your fellow Americans the right to vote in this country.

There is no issue of state's rights or national rights. There is only the struggle for human rights. I have not the slightest doubt what will be your answer. But the last time a President sent a civil rights bill to the Congress it contained a provision to protect voting rights in Federal elections. That civil rights bill was passed after eight long months of debate. And when that bill came to my desk from the Congress for signature, the heart of the voting provision had been eliminated.

This time, on this issue, there must be no delay, or no hesitation, or no compromise with our purpose. We cannot, we must not, refuse to protect the right of every American to vote in every election that he may desire to participate in."

53. What connection can be made between the civil rights protests and the passing of the Voting Rights Act of 1965?

a. The civil rights protests drew attention to the issue of voting rights, and this led to President Johnson enacting the Voting Rights Act of 1965.
b. The civil rights protests caused issues that delayed the passing of the Voting Rights Act of 1965.
c. The civil rights protests were prompted by the passing of the Voting Rights Act of 1965.
d. The civil rights protests ended issues with voting rights, which made the passing of the Voting Rights Act of 1965 symbolic rather than necessary.

Refer to the following for questions 54–56:

In many states, the state legislature has control over redistricting both state legislative and congressional districts. A majority vote is required to pass district lines, and the first draft of the redistricting legislation is created by a committee. These bills can be overridden by legislators and vetoed by the governor. A few states—Maryland, Mississippi, and Florida—leave the gubernatorial veto out of the process.

Redistricting is completed every 10 years, after the decennial census. The way in which these district lines are drawn can have a big impact on elections, including how communities are represented and how political power is spread out. Because communities and populations change over time, the redistricting process is important for ensuring that districts are equally populated and representative of the population of the state. A technique called *gerrymandering* can be used in favor of or opposition to one party or politician. One method of gerrymandering is to split up groups of people who have similar characteristics into different districts so that their voting power is weakened. A district that has been gerrymandered sometimes looks irregular, but this is not always the case.

Most cases of gerrymandering are partisan. One method is racial gerrymandering, used to minimize the voting impact of particular racial groups. Negative racial gerrymandering involves redistricting to keep racial minorities from electing their preferred candidate. The Voting Rights Act of 1980 is meant to make districts redraw their lines if they have a discriminatory effect. Computers can be used to create fair district lines, but they can also be used to create gerrymandered districts using the information from the census.

54. Which of the following is another technique that would cause gerrymandering?

a. Drawing district lines to include smaller groups of people
b. Leaving the entire state as one large district
c. Redistricting the state every two years instead of every 10 years
d. Putting certain groups of voters into as few districts as possible

55. Which of the following would be a likely result of creating an even grid of district lines throughout a state rather than creating district lines based on the census?

a. The districts would alternate between the two major political parties.
b. The districts would be representative of the demographics of the state.
c. The districts would all have different populations.
d. The districts would include all minorities in one grid square.

56. Which of the following is the best definition of the word *partisan*?

a. Favoring a particular political party or candidate
b. Legal to enact in most states
c. Ethical to arrange depending on the motivation
d. Generated by computers to create fair divisions

Refer to the following for questions 57–58:

An exchange rate is the relative value of one currency compared to another. The most often referenced currency is the US dollar, so exchange rates are often in terms of equivalence to one US dollar or the number of US dollars equal one unit of the other currency. This chart shows the exchange rates by year for the US dollar (USD) versus euros (EUR). When more of a currency is required to buy the same amount of another currency, it means that the first currency has appreciated. The exchange rate can affect the movement of money between countries.

USD to EUR Exchange Rates by Year

Year	Rate
2017	0.923
2018	0.848
2019	0.893
2020	0.877
2021	0.846
2022	0.951

57. Which of the following is the best measure of central tendency for these exchange rates?

a. Mean only
b. Median and mean
c. Median and mode
d. Median only

58. If the exchange rate in 2016 was 0.75, which of the following would best characterize trade in 2016 versus trade in 2017 between the US and the European Union?

a. The US would have stopped exporting goods to countries in the European Union in 2016 and resumed in 2017.
b. Countries in the European Union would have purchased fewer exports from the US in 2016 than in 2017.
c. This would not have affected trade between the US and countries in the European Union.
d. Countries in the European Union would have purchased more exports from the US in 2016 than in 2017.

Refer to the following for question 59:

The following is an excerpt from Barack Obama's keynote address at the Democratic National Convention in 2004. At this time, he was a senator delivering a speech in support of the Democratic Party nominee, John Kerry. In 2008, Obama was elected president and became the first African American president.

> "On behalf of the great state of Illinois, crossroads of a nation, land of Lincoln, let me express my deep gratitude for the privilege of addressing this convention. Tonight is a particular honor for me because, let's face it, my presence on this stage is pretty unlikely. My father was a foreign student, born and raised in a small village in Kenya. He grew up herding goats, went to school in a tin-roof shack. His father, my grandfather, was a cook, a domestic servant.
>
> But my grandfather had larger dreams for his son. Through hard work and perseverance my father got a scholarship to study in a magical place: America, which stood as a beacon of freedom and opportunity to so many who had come before. While studying here, my father met my mother. She was born in a town on the other side of the world, in Kansas. Her father worked on oil rigs and farms through most of the Depression. The day after Pearl Harbor he signed up for duty, joined Patton's army and marched across Europe. Back home, my grandmother raised their baby and went to work on a bomber assembly line. After the war, they studied on the GI Bill, bought a house through FHA, and moved west in search of opportunity.
>
> ...
>
> I stand here today, grateful for the diversity of my heritage, aware that my parents' dreams live on in my precious daughters. I stand here knowing that my story is part of the larger American story, that I owe a debt to all of those who came before me, and that, in no other country on earth, is my story even possible. Tonight, we gather to affirm the greatness of our nation, not because of the height of our skyscrapers, or the power of our military, or the size of our economy. Our pride is based on a very simple premise, summed up in a declaration made over two hundred years ago, "We hold these truths to be self-evident, that all men are created

equal. That they are endowed by their Creator with certain inalienable rights. That among these are life, liberty and the pursuit of happiness."

59. Which of the following best describes how historical context shaped Obama's assertions in this speech?

a. Since many Americans before him had attained similar accomplishments, it was not difficult for him to achieve the same as they did.
b. Because his background was full of difficulties, he no longer believed equality was possible in the US.
c. Since America, like most countries, had long ago committed to equality, he hesitated to mention his background in his speech.
d. Due to the progress already made toward equality in the US, his family's background was not a barrier to his current position.

60. What is one conclusion that can be made from this chart?

Statistics from the US Bureau of Labor

a. High US unemployment in 1929 was a cause of the Great Depression.
b. US unemployment was higher in the early 1930s than unemployment in other countries.
c. High US unemployment showed a small decrease. Then, it held steady in the early 1930s.
d. The Great Depression caused a sharp increase in the rate of unemployment in the US.

Answer Key and Explanations for Test #1

Language Arts–Reading

1. C: Point of view refers to the vantage point from which a story is written. First person uses the pronoun *I*. Second person uses the pronoun *you*. Third person uses the pronouns *he/she/they*. There is no fourth-person point of view. This passage was written in the third person.

2. B: The words *mysterious* and *important* used in the sentence help the reader deduce that Jo looked secretive. Jo did not look jubilant (joyful), disheveled (disarrayed), or angry.

3. C: The last sentence states that Laurie was "an incorrigible tease." From this statement you can infer that Laurie was unruly or unmanageable. *Stoic* means not showing passion or emotion. *Taciturn* means silent. *Uncanny* means supernatural. There is nothing in the passage to imply he had any of these characteristics.

4. C: The passage is expository because it communicates information about the mysteries of the Bermuda Triangle and what researchers have studied and now believe. The author includes facts to inform the reader, which is the goal of expository writing. The passage does not tell a story or describe one event, so it is not a narrative. The passage also does not seek to lead the reader to take action or accept a particular conclusion, so this passage is not persuasive. The passage also does not give technical information and does not aim to help the reader understand a technical concept, so this passage is not technical.

5. D: Choice D is the best summary statement for the entire passage because it clearly describes what the author is saying about the results of studies on the Bermuda Triangle. Each paragraph in the passage includes details that support the statement that researchers have never found anything truly mysterious about the Bermuda Triangle. Choices A, B, and C are all details found in the passage, but none of these choices give a summary of the whole passage. Each of these answer choices support the statement in choice D, as do the rest of the details in the passage.

6. A: Of all the sentences provided, choice A is the one with which the author would most likely agree. The passage suggests that most of the "mysteries" of the Bermuda Triangle can be explained in a reasonable way. The passage mentions that some expand the Triangle to the Azores, but this is a point of fact, and the author makes no mention of whether or not this is in error. The author quotes the Navy's response to the disappearance of the planes, but there is no reason to believe the author questions this response. The author raises questions about the many myths surrounding the Triangle, but at no point does the author claim that these myths are to blame for the accidents that fall "within the expected margin of error."

7. B: A collection of travel journal entries from someone who frequently traveled the Bermuda Triangle is the most likely of these choices to provide detailed information. Choice A would provide useful information, but this information is not likely to go into much detail. Choice C would likely include many details, but it would only contain information about a very small section of the Bermuda Triangle. Choice D could include details about the Bermuda Triangle, but these details would also only describe a limited section of the area and would be given through a narrow perspective.

8. D: In the first paragraph, Miss Lucas states that "so very fine a young man, with family, fortune, everything in his favour, should think highly of himself. If I may so express it, he has a *right* to be proud." Basically, she feels he deserves to be proud because he is physically attractive, comes from a good family, has money, and is successful.

9. A: This question is asking you to make an inference about Elizabeth's feeling towards the gentleman. In paragraph 2, Elizabeth is "mortified" by the gentleman's actions towards her. From this statement, you can make the inference that she was offended by his actions.

10. C: Theme is a message or lesson conveyed by a written text. The message is usually about life, society, or human nature. This particular excerpt is exploring pride as it relates to human nature. Mary's observations on pride are the best summary of the theme of this passage. "By all that I have ever read, I am convinced that it is very common indeed, that human nature is particularly prone to it." The best answer is choice C.

11. C: Paragraph 3 gives the answer to this question. According to Mary, pride is an opinion of yourself, and vanity is what we want others to think of us.

12. B: In the first paragraph of the essay, the author characterizes amateurs as "an elite group within the music scene" and states that there are several "technological, demographic, and economic factors" that account for them doing better than professionals. The tone of the essay is documentary—the author doesn't make any judgments about whether this is a good development or a bad one. He simply states that amateurs are more successful relative to professionals than they have been before and goes on to examine the reasons for this. Therefore, choice B is correct.

13. D: The key is the phrase *directly support*. The essay needs to come right out and say the correct answer, not imply that it is true. Paragraph 3 says that digital file sharing "robs the professionals of what has traditionally been one of their biggest sources of revenue." Paragraph 2 provides less direct evidence, saying that many clubs that were once able to pay professionals now can't. Professionals have lost most of their income from both small clubs and recordings. Therefore, choice D is correct.

14. B: The second sentence in the final paragraph is a giveaway. If the "amateurs are the only ones who can afford to buy new gear and fix broken equipment, keep their cars in working order to get to shows, and pay to promote their shows," then the professionals must not be able to do any of those things, as stated in choice B.

15. C: The essay as a whole discusses how the current musical scene negatively affects professional musicians while leaving amateurs unharmed. The second paragraph, for example, discusses how professionals are no longer able to make a living playing small venues and must "fight more desperately than ever for those few lucrative gigs." The final paragraph states that, because of the effect on their finances, professionals are unable to maintain the gear and transportation they need to "keep the higher-paying gigs." It goes on to say that "a fairly skilled amateur . . . will be able to fake his way through most of what a professional does . . . to play professional shows." Therefore, professionals are falling behind amateurs at small venues (which professionals can't afford to play because of the lack of pay) and at professional gigs (where professionals can't play because they can't afford professional gear). Therefore, choice C is correct.

16. C: The Constitution overrides state law in some cases. Answer choices B and D are quite obviously factually incorrect. The last choice, A, is also not stated or implied in the passage, but this answer might seem correct to someone who hadn't read the passage carefully.

17. A: Although state courts exercised judicial review prior to the ratification of the Constitution, the doctrine is most often traced to the landmark US Supreme Court decision *Marbury v. Madison*

(1803), which struck down an act of Congress as unconstitutional. This sentence means that laws passed by Congress must comply with the Constitution. None of the other choices do.

18. A: This is an informational passage about history, so *historical* could be used to describe its contents. None of the other words fit this passage. *Introspective* refers to a passage that describes a person's internal thoughts or considerations. *Prospective* refers to the future. And *demonstrative* refers to expressing feeling or emotion.

19. A: *Ratification* in the context of this passage refers to an endorsement. For example, when the 13 Colonies ratified the Constitution, they endorsed it.

20. D: When Oliver Wendell Holmes dissented from many opinions, it meant he disagreed with the majority on the court. Therefore, his opinion was contradictory.

21. C: As the passage explains, the Supreme Court's ruling in the 1803 case of *Marbury v. Madison*, which invalidated a law passed by Congress on the grounds that it violated the Constitution, is the foundation of the legal concept of judicial review.

22. B: In the second sentence, the phrase *so long had sleep been denied to her* tells us she had been prevented from sleeping for some time. Someone who has not slept for a very long time might start to believe that they would never be able to sleep again, and so would be surprised to wake up.

23. D: The text tells us she was "feigning," which means pretending, regarding whether or not she was asleep. This is further clarified by saying that "he was not fooled," indicating that she was trying to convince Garth that she was still asleep.

24. A: Despite his ugliness and deformities, Garth is a gentle soul who wants to be accepted as a friend by the girl.

25. D: At first repelled by the sight of Garth in the window, the girl eventually expresses pity when she learns that he is also deaf.

26. B: Garth's deformities are repugnant to her at first, and she must overcome this emotion. The phrase *steeling herself*, as used in the passage, means that she was mentally preparing herself to do something difficult, in this case to look at someone she found revolting in appearance.

27. B: Garth seems to know that the girl does not want to look at him, as he tells her that he is hidden from sight, and his voice is described as plaintive and pained. When the girl first looks out the window, Garth looks grief-stricken and resigned, which indicates that he was sad about the situation but knows that she does not want to interact with him.

28. B: The text tells us that he sees her lips move and thinks that that she is sending him away rather than asking him to come closer. He is already full of negative emotions and does not immediately understand that she is willing to speak with him.

29. D: *Supplicating* means to ask or beg for something earnestly or humbly. In this case, Garth nervously looks up at the girl, begging with her his eyes to see past his deformities and become kind to him.

30. D: The passage is very clear that the girl at first finds Garth revolting because of his physical appearance. She has to make a lot of effort to even look at him, and so it is surprising that she gets to the point of being able to touch him within moments of this first look.

31. D: The girl quickly understands Garth's sadness about his own condition and sympathizes with him. She is willing to look past his appearance and connect with him emotionally.

32. C: The passage presents several pieces of evidence that Garth resents his life. He is presented as so deformed that other people are frequently repelled and try to avoid contact with him. The passage uses various words to indicate Garth's feelings, including the following: pained, grief-stricken, resigned, despairing, and bitter. Contemplative is another possible choice, but it does not do a good job of capturing Garth's sadness and bitterness at his condition. Despite being sad, Garth would not be considered destitute, as he is not starving or without his basic needs being met. The word *deflated* carries the impression that air has been let out of something that should be full of air. Think of a car tire or a balloon in which the air has been suddenly let out. Garth does not seem to be deflated, as he seems to be constantly sad and likely has been for a long time. In fact, the story indicates that he is the happiest that he can remember being.

33. D: The girl has shown that she sympathizes with him by taking his arm, and Garth feels that he is being accepted despite his deformities.

34. C: The tricky thing about this question is that all the choices are true statements about things said in the essay. Only one, however, is the main idea. The best way to find it is to go to the first paragraph. In it, the author calls the ability to tell true and false statements apart "one of the main goals of every police officer." He goes further, calling this ability "the only way to punish the guilty, exonerate the innocent, and do the most possible good in preventing future crimes." Choice C, therefore, is the correct answer.

35. A: If there is one point that the author has repeated many times in this article, it is that police need to be able to investigate lies to conduct investigations. Therefore, choice A is the correct answer.

36. C: In paragraph 2, the author states that "smoke" lies "slow down an investigation." Therefore, Choice C is the correct response.

37. B: This passage is clearly intended for a non-expert adult readership. It uses language that general readers can understand, and uses a reference to a Charles Dickens character that readers of the time might be familiar with (Mr. Micawber in the novel *David Copperfield*) to illustrate its point. Economists certainly understand economy better than Barnum (the author) does and so would not need this explanation, and there is nothing in the passage to indicate that Barnum is specifically writing for teachers or philanthropists.

38. D: The author suggests that many people who believe that they understand how to become wealthy in fact do not, and that he knows better than they do. The word *patronizing* means condescending, or talking down to someone. The author implies that he understands economy better than most of his readers despite it being so simple that everyone should understand it.

39. A: The passage explains a problem that most people have: the inability to earn more money than they spend. It seems clear that the author is about to describe the correct means of personal economy. This, combined with the title *The Art of Money-Getting*, only make sense as part of a book or manual intended to explain how people can improve their own lives. While it may contain stories from the author's own life, it is not primarily an autobiography. An epistle is a letter or series of letters, and this excerpt is not a letter. It is also not a novel, which is a work of fiction.

40. B: The passage mentions that handwriting notes can, on occasion, be more reliable than using a recording device during an interview (B). The passage also mentions that it can be difficult to take notes quickly and legibly. In other words, note taking can be slow (A), and handwritten notes may be difficult to read after the interview (D). The first paragraph states that relying on handwritten notes during an interview can distract journalists and cause them to look away from the person they are interviewing (C).

41. A: In the passage, the first paragraph gives two examples of body language when it describes an interview subject closing his eyes and trembling sightly. This implies that body language consists of nonverbal, physical cues. A shocked look (B), wringing hands (C), and a glance (D) are all examples of body language, because they are nonverbal, physical actions. Answering a question quietly is not an example of body language because it is a verbal response (A).

42. D: Choice D states that wise journalists both record audio and take hand-written notes during interviews so that they have a backup resource in case the recording or notes are not reliable. Choice A simply states the purpose of recording devices but does not give enough information to support the conclusion that journalists should both record audio and take notes. Choices B and C show that audio recordings are not always reliable, but neither of these choices shows why it is a good practice to both record audio and take notes.

43. B: In the opening paragraph, Burke cautions the reader to wait to congratulate people on their freedom until he or she can see beyond the turmoil and emotions and judge whether this freedom is actually "a blessing." While he does call liberty a strong principle, he advises caution on admiring it. He also advises caution in congratulating those who have just found liberty. His reference to avoiding judgment was not in reference to different cultures and their preferred freedoms, but a general statement about understanding what newly won freedom really was.

44. D: Burke uses the analogy of liquor to explain how people could not think rationally in the early excitement of liberty. He was not referring to literal liquor (A, B). While it did have the connotation of obscuring the truth, there is no reference to darkness (C).

45. C: Choice C is the correct answer because the author of Passage 1, Edmund Burke, argues that it would be unwise to celebrate the new liberty in France without a longer, deeper assessment of how it has been combined with the various elements of governance, including government, public force, army discipline, revenue collection, morality and religion, property stability, peace, order, and civil and social manners. The author does not advocate for showing quick support or ignoring the impact of new freedoms on various aspects of society. The author would argue that one cannot accurately judge the strength of a principle without observing the long-standing effects of the principle.

46. C: Burke spends the entire passage warning against revolting without a clear idea of what victory would look like, and Paine also mentions the importance of careful forethought rather than being led by emotions. Neither indicates that liberty is the highest gift a person can be given, though Paine does consider it very important. Paine makes the point that the King may love his people while the laws are still corrupt, but Burke makes no mention of this. Paine also indicates that the French government was corrupt and action was necessary, but Burke does not concede that anything was necessary other than caution before action.

47. A: Paine advocates the overthrow of the government rather than its reform, claiming that its despotic principles were "too deeply rooted to be removed" except by revolution. Paine does not claim that the nation would not survive without change. Paine specifically states that the revolution is not against Louis XVI. Paine refers to the principles that are centuries old but makes no reference to laws that may be inappropriate for the current generation of French people.

48. B: In Paragraph 4 of Passage 2, Paine states that Burke does not "attend to the distinction between men and principles." In other words, he does not understand that revolting against a corrupt government is not synonymous with rejecting a king. Paine does not argue that liberty should be obtained at any cost; rather, he comments that many other revolutions were inspired by hatred instead of good motives. Paine does refer to the king's regard for his people but does not indicate that Burke is unaware of this. And while Paine does urge acting "with determined vigor" in the crisis, he again does not indicate that Burke is unaware.

49. C: Burke argues in the first paragraph of Passage 1 that the emotions of the revolution make it difficult to judge rationally. He does not make any mention of human rights. He mentions that the real movers are not always the ones who "appear the most stirring," but he does not imply that those who contemplated the revolution were not the movers.

50. B: Paine rebuts Burke's work by pointing out what he believed to be a flaw in Burke's reasoning. This evidence is neither new nor merely looking at it from a different angle. Finally, Paine is not supporting Burke's premise.

Language Arts–Writing

1. B: The part of the sentence "who says that..." is a parenthetical phrase about Richard Louv, not about the subject of the sentence. The *and who* is therefore incorrect, and the phrase needs to be set off from the sentence by a comma.

2. B: The best answer is (B) because it best captures the logical connection of the sentences: the fear of abduction is the reason that parents are afraid to let kids play in the woods.

3. D: The sentence needs a subject. Answer (D) is the one that most clearly identifies a subject.

4. D: The word *this* most logically refers to child abduction. Although not stated explicitly, it is the only choice that could logically be described as "a terrible thing" and "very rare."

5. B: Although the paragraph does not make its point explicitly, it clearly states that kids are spending too much time with video games and TV (being entertained by technology) and would be helped by more time getting their feet and hands dirty and touching things rather than just reading about them (having a positive sensory experience of nature).

6. A: The sentence "Many people have proposed explanations for this drop" provides an introduction to the short explanations that follow. It should come after the first sentence.

7. C: The adverb *particularly* clearly modifies the adjectival phrase *well known*, and no hyphen is needed. Choice B subtly changes the meaning. Choice D corrects the spelling of the original but is a more awkward phrasing.

8. C: Choice C eliminates the slang expression *what with*. Choice D subtly changes the meaning.

9. B: Choice A reads poorly and fails to fully connect why the artists did not see his work. Choice C fails to make the connection with the preceding sentence, establishing itself as the explanation for Daumier's lack of influence, and choice D fails to explain why other artists did not see Daumier's work.

10. B: Since the sentence begins with "This is also true," the clause in choice B is redundant with the preceding sentence. None of the other choices address this.

11. A: Choice A expands upon the previous sentence by explaining why he is considered the greatest sculptor of the era.

12. D: The word *however* shows that the sentence will provide a contrast to the preceding sentence. Choice B does this as well, but it repeats the same expression used three sentences before.

13. C: The adverb *internationally* modifies the adjective *recognized*. Therefore, choice C has the best grammar and flow. Choice A has *internationally* incorrectly modifying *passports*. Choice B misplaces the adverb *internationally* after the word *documents*. Choice D has a singular pronoun modifying a plural noun.

14. D: Choice D has the necessary commas. Choice A is lacking commas after *grant* and *issue*. Choice B needs an additional comma after *issue*. Choice C incorrectly capitalizes *passports*.

15. D: The sentences should be joined by a comma to make one sentence, which choice D does. Choice A is wrong because there are two sentences, but the word *and* indicates a continuation of the idea. Choice B incorrectly uses a colon. A semicolon is used when there are two independent ideas, which is not the case in choice C.

16. C: The sentence in choice C flows better than the other choices and correctly uses a comma for an interrupter. Choice A does not flow. Choice B lacks the necessary comma. Choice D is not corrected by adding commas and still reads poorly.

17. B: Choice B is correct because both *books* and *cards* should be plural. Choice A lacks the plural *cards*. Choice C is incorrect because the verb *issue* is in the plural form rather than the singular form. Choice D is incorrect because there is no reason for the word *use* to be in a possessive form.

18. C: Choice C is the best choice for the context. Choice B repeats sentence 8. Choices A and D, while true, don't provide any information that is pertinent to sentence 11.

19. B: The third sentence of this passage refers to "these insecticides," but there is no earlier reference to any insecticides in the paragraph. The sentence, "Insects that carry the disease can develop resistance to the chemicals, or insecticides, that are used to kill the mosquitoes," needs to be placed after sentence 2 for sentence 3 to make sense.

20. D: There should be a comma after *November 30*. Choice A is incorrect because the second sentence has no verb and is thus incomplete. Choice B incorrectly places a comma after *season*. Choice C uses a semicolon incorrectly.

21. B: The beginning of the sentence is in the present tense, so the verb in the second part of the sentence should be *includes*. Choices A and D are wrong because they both use verbs in the past tense. Choice C is incorrect because the verb is in the future tense.

22. A: Choice A is punctuated correctly. Choice B is incorrect because the order of information does not flow in the sentence. Choice C uses a semicolon incorrectly. Choice D places a comma in the wrong place.

23. B: Choice B is correct because it adds information similar to the theme of the passage. Choice C basically says the same thing as sentence 9. Choices A and D are technically correct, but they do not follow the theme of the passage.

24. C: The preposition *when* indicates a relation of time. Choice A is incorrect because there is no joining relation. Choice B is incorrect because it uses the wrong time relation. Choice D does not indicate a time relation.

25. B: Choice A incorrectly places the primary thought of the sentence second. Choice C is awkwardly written and lacks a comma after the first *hurricanes*. Choice D uses the incorrect verb form *includes*.

26. B: Choice B is the best choice because it correctly transitions from sentence 7 to sentence 8 and maintains the author's original meaning.

27. C: In terms of determining their validity, hypotheses are confirmed or disconfirmed. None of the other options are meaningful.

28. D: Since the sentence begins in the present tense, it should continue in the present tense as well. The proper verb to be used in this clause is *affect*, meaning to have an impact, not *effect*, meaning to bring about.

29. B: The second sentence of the same paragraph states, "In the monkey example, every single monkey in the history of monkeys would need to be examined before the hypothesis could be proven or disproven." In the passage's last sentence, "...infinite sample sets for confirmation or disconfirmation" refers directly to that second sentence (quoted above here). The initial sentence of this paragraph (A) states that evidence-based hypotheses must use probability because sample sets are too large, which agrees with the sentence following it, but it does not specifically identify infinite sample sets as the sentence following it does. The fourth sentence of the previous paragraph (C) shows how even one piece of evidence out of a very large—but NOT infinite—sample size of one billion can disprove a hypothesis rather than showing how infinite sample sizes are required.

30. C: Choice C correctly uses a comma after *trick or treat*. Choice A is incorrect because there is no comma after *trick or treat*. Choice B is not the correct choice because it does not have quotation marks around *trick or treat* to identify what the children are calling out. Choice D incorrectly places a comma after *doors*.

31. D: Choice D correctly uses the pronoun *who*, which agrees with *adults*. Choices A and B respectively use the incorrect pronouns *that* and *which*. Choice C is incorrect because a comma would be needed after the opening phrase *just as much as children*.

32. C: Choice C makes sense in terms of the statement. Choices A and B suggest an opposite relationship, which does not fit in with the first sentence. Choice D would create an example before establishing the thought necessary for explanation and is thus incorrect.

33. A: The ideas in choice A flow logically. Choice B is awkward. Choices C and D do not make sense.

34. C: By adding the preposition *into* in choice C, the sentence makes sense. Choice A is incorrect because it does not use a preposition. Choice B incorrectly uses the word *pressures*. Choice D is incorrect because the word *hasty* does not require the article *an* in front of it.

35. D: The main idea is *shop*, so putting it at the beginning of the sentence makes it flow the best. Choice A puts it at the end, which dilutes its importance. Choice B incorrectly places commas before and after *shop around*. Choice C would require a comma after *showrooms* to make it correct.

36. B: Choice B conveys the correct meaning of the sentence. Choice A uses the singular form of *service* when the plural form is needed. Choice C incorrectly places commas after *services* both times it appears. Choice D has the contraction *You'll* together with *may*. There can be one or the other, but not both.

37. B: Choice B places the comma correctly between *margin* and *which*. Choice A needs a comma before *which*. Choice C makes no sense, and choice D is awkwardly worded.

38. C: By putting the secondary idea of a monthly payment in parentheses, thereby omitting the *and* from the sentence by using a pronoun, the sentence reads very well. Choices A, B and D use dashes, commas, or a combination of the two, all of which result in poor readability.

39. C: Sentence 4, regarding Jefferson's affair with one of his slaves, is not directly relevant to the main topic at hand, which is Jefferson's debts.

40. B: Choice B is correct because it replaces the incorrect adverb *possibly* with the correct adjective *possible*. Choice A incorrectly uses the adverb *possibly*. Choice C uses the correct adjective, but the verb *can* does not go with the sense of possibility because it is too definite. Choice D is incorrect because the article *a* is not placed before the noun *possibility*.

41. C: Choice C is correct because it uses the preposition *with*, which indicates *as a result*. Choice A incorrectly uses the preposition *from*, which indicates a starting place. Choice B uses the incorrect prepositions *from* and *within*. Choice D incorrectly uses *then*, which indicates *next* rather than a possibility.

42. A: Choice A uses the correct verb form. Choices B, C, and D all use incorrect forms of the verb.

43. D: Choice D correctly uses a plural verb (*eliminate*) and pronoun (*their*) that agree with the subject *those*, which refers to banks, and a comma to connect the introductory clause to the rest of the sentence. Choice A is incorrect because the singular verb *eliminates* and pronoun *its* do not agree with the plural *those*. Choice B also uses the wrong form of the verb and incorrectly uses a semicolon after *services*. Choice C uses the wrong preposition *within* along with the incorrect verb and pronoun forms.

44. B: The verb *might be* indicates a probability. Choice A is incorrect since the verb *must be* means something is necessary and has to be done, which is not the case here. Choice C is awkwardly written. In choice D, the verb *have chosen* does not agree with the verb tense of the earlier verb *might be*.

45. A: Choice A is correct because it uses *In both cases* at the beginning of the sentence rather than at the end like choice B does. Choice C incorrectly uses the adverb *then* instead of the preposition *than*. Choice D incorrectly uses the adjective *any* when the previous sentences have two subjects.

46. A: Choice A is the only option with the correct verb form. Choice B uses a plural verb form rather than a singular. Choice C has a verb in a past tense, but *now* makes it clear that the sentence is in the present tense. Choice D has an incorrect verb form as well.

47. A: Choice A uses the possessive form *Forest Service's* correctly. Choice B has no possessive and also has an incorrect verb form. Choice C uses an incorrect possessive form, and choice D has a plural noun *milestones* with a singular article *a*.

48. D: Choice A does not have *legacy* capitalized as it should be. Choice B does not have the proper name *Forest Legacy* capitalized. Choice C incorrectly capitalizes *The* and does not capitalize *legacy*.

49. B: Choice B has a logical flow of ideas. Choices A, C, and D are all awkwardly written.

50. B: Sentence 2, regarding Feynman's musicianship, is of little relevance to the discussion of the atomic theory.

51. C: We can see from the other sentences in this paragraph that each is written in present perfect tense. To match these, we need to choose a term with *has* or *have*. Choice A is past tense and choices B and D are present tense, so they are incorrect.

52. D: As written (A), the sentence has a dangling modifier (because the subject of *tracing back millennia* should be *calendars*, but the way the sentence is written the subject is, incorrectly, *archaeologists*). Choice B has the correct subject, but is written in passive voice. Additionally, it is written in past tense rather than present perfect, which does not fit with the rest of the paragraph. Choice C is also written in passive voice, and it does not end with a comma, which indicates that the archaeologists, not the calendars, are showing the ancient views of movement and time. Only choice D is straightforward and grammatically correct.

53. B: As written, the sentence is a comma splice because each clause is a complete sentence and needs to be joined by a semicolon. The last two choices are convoluted and potentially confusing. Only the second choice is both grammatically correct and clear.

54. C: This paragraph discusses solar and lunisolar calendars. It is transitioning from the previous paragraph, which discussed the ancient lunar calendar found in Scotland, so the introduction should acknowledge the old subject while introducing the new one. Choice A refers to the previous paragraph, but the detail used (Scotland) is not relevant to the subject of solar calendars. Choice B introduces the idea of solar calendars but does not transition from the previous paragraph. Choice D refers to the previous paragraph, but the wording is awkward and confusing. Choice C refers back to the previous paragraph while setting up the contrast for the current paragraph.

55. A: The word *lunisolar* indicates a combination of *lunar* and *solar*, and we can confirm this combination by reading the next sentence in the passage. Choice B is incorrect because it indicates only one, choice C is incorrect because it indicates zero, and choice D is incorrect because it leaves the possibility of only one.

56. B: The parenthetical phrase is a nonrestrictive clause. In other words, the sentence is complete and makes sense without it. The word *which* is the proper choice with nonrestrictive clauses. A restrictive clause, on the other hand, would use *that*. Neither *how* nor *what* make grammatical sense in this context.

57. D: The sentence is referring to the lunisolar calendar, which is based on both solar and lunar measurements. Using *however* (A, B) or *although* (C) provides contradiction rather than agreement.

58. C: This sentence discusses the way Roman politicians adjusted the calendar to reflect political goals. The best term for this is *skewed*. To say that it was *stabilized* (A) would reflect the opposite. The Romans did not rename (B) or tear (D) the calendar.

59. D: This story about the Egyptian astronomer adds an interesting fact, but it does not contribute meaningful information or provide supporting details to the main points. It is true that this is the best position in the paragraph, following up on the political problem (A), but this does not warrant keeping it in the paragraph. This sentence is not a response to the priests' mistake of too many leap days, so the end of the paragraph would not be the best position (B). The fact that solar calendars have been previously discussed is not a reason to remove it (C), as the solar calendar is one of the main ideas and is mentioned multiple times.

60. D: Because this clause is preceded by a comma rather than a semicolon, it cannot be an independent clause. Choices B and C are incorrect because they create independent clauses (stand-alone sentences) and therefore lead to comma splice sentences. Choice A is incorrect because it is missing verbiage to make the sentence grammatically correct: it either needs a subject or a conjunction. The participle form provides a grammatically correct opening to the clause.

Essay Question

1. Essay question graders commonly look for the following elements in a strong response: strong content knowledge, clear organization, and effective arguments or examples. Language and usage are not usually strictly graded, but can make a big impact on the clarity of your ideas.

Please use the provided rubric to make sure your response meets these common criteria. Try to have a friend or family member grade your response for you or take a break after writing your response and return to grade it with fresh eyes.

Constructed Response Rubric

Domain	Description
Content Knowledge	• The response directly addresses every part of the prompt. • The response demonstrates independent knowledge of the topic. • The response discusses the topic at an appropriate depth.
Organization	• The response introduces the topic, usually with a thesis statement or by restating the prompt. • The response directly addresses the prompt by providing a clear and concise answer or solution. • The answer or solution is supported by logical arguments or evidence. • The response restates the main idea in the conclusion.
Arguments and Examples	• The response provides a reasonable answer to the prompt. • The answer is supported by strong reasoning or evidence. • The response develops ideas logically and connects ideas to one another. • The reasoning and evidence provided act to support a unified main idea.
Language and Usage	• The response demonstrates effective use of grammar and uses varied sentence structure throughout the response. • The response demonstrates correct use of spelling, punctuation, and capitalization. • The response demonstrates strong and varied use of vocabulary relevant to the topic and appropriate for the intended audience.

Mathematics

1. C: To determine this, first solve for x. Start by subtracting 2 from both sides.

$$10x + 2 = 7$$
$$10x = 5$$

Then, divide both sides by 10.

$$x = \frac{5}{10} = \frac{1}{2}$$

Since $x = \frac{1}{2}$, multiply this by 2 to find that $2x = 2\left(\frac{1}{2}\right) = 1$.

2. D: If the first lap takes 50 seconds, the second one takes 20% more, or $T_2 = 1.2 \times T_1 = 1.2 \times 50 = 60$ seconds, where T_1 and T_2 are the times required for the first and second laps, respectively. Similarly, the time required for the third lap is $T_3 = 1.2 \times T_2 = 1.2 \times 60 = 72$ seconds. To find the total time, add the times for the three laps together: $50 + 60 + 72 = 182$ seconds.

3. A: To solve, first figure out how much space remains once her car is in the garage. $19 \text{ feet} - 15 \text{ feet} = 4 \text{ feet}$. To center the car, she should park halfway between the remaining space. Therefore, her car would need to be parked 2 feet from the front of the garage for it to be centered.

4. C: A system of linear equations can be solved by using matrices or by using the graphing, substitution, or elimination (also called linear combination) method. The elimination method is shown here:

$$3x + 4y = 2$$
$$2x + 6y = -2$$

In order to eliminate x by linear combination, multiply the top equation by 2 and the bottom equation by −3 so that the coefficients of the x-terms will be additive inverses.

$$2(3x + 4y = 2)$$
$$-3(2x + 6y = -2)$$

Then, add the two equations and solve for y.

$$6x + 8y = 4$$
$$\underline{-6x - 18y = 6}$$
$$-10y = 10$$
$$y = -1$$

Substitute −1 for y in either of the given equations and solve for x.

$$3x + 4y = 2$$
$$3x + 4(-1) = 2$$
$$3x - 4 = 2$$
$$3x = 6$$
$$x = 2$$

The solution to the system of equations is $(2, -1)$.

5. B: The stock first increased by 10%, or \$10 (10% of \$100), to \$110 per share. Then, the price decreased by \$11 (10% of \$110) so that the sell price was $\$110 - \$11 = \$99$ per share, and the sell price for 50 shares was $\$99 \times \$50 = \$4{,}950$.

6. D: The sides of a triangle must all be greater than 0. The sum of the lengths of the two shorter sides must be greater than the length of the third side. Since we are looking for the minimum value of the perimeter, assume the longer of the two given sides, which is 6, is the longest side of the triangle. Then, the third side must be greater than $6 - 4 = 2$. Since we are told the sides are all integers, the last side must be 3 units in length. Thus, the minimum length for the perimeter is $4 + 6 + 3 = 13$ units.

7. C: If \$70, the amount used to buy more lemons, represents 35% of Herbert's earnings, then 1% corresponds to $\frac{\$70}{35} = \$2$. To determine how much profit he takes home, multiply the dollar amount that represents 1%, which is \$2, by 15 to get $\$2 \times 15 = \$30$. Therefore, Herbert takes home \$30 in profit.

8. C: She has been working at the rate of 10 papers per hour. She has 30 papers remaining and must grade them in the 2.5 hours that she has left, which corresponds to a rate of 12 papers per hour. $\frac{12}{10} = 120\%$ of her previous rate, or 20% faster.

9. D: The ratio of the ruler's height to the distance from eye to ruler, which is the tangent of the angle subtended at the eye by the ruler's height, must be the same as the ratio of the lighthouse's height to its distance from the eye, which is the tangent of the same angle. Since 3 in $= \frac{1}{4}$ ft, we have $\frac{\frac{1}{4}}{2} = \frac{60}{D}$. Solving for D gives $D = \frac{2\times 60}{\frac{1}{4}} = 120 \times 4 = 480$. Therefore, the lighthouse is 480 feet away.

10. D: Start by solving the equation as you typically would until you isolate the x^2 on one side.

$$x^2 - 4 = 45$$
$$x^2 = 49$$

When you take the square root of a number, the answer is the positive and negative values of the root. Therefore, $x = 7$ and $x = -7$. Since only –7 is an answer choice, that is the correct answer.

11. A: The first two prime numbers larger than 10 are 11 and 13, and their product is 143. The largest prime number smaller than 30 is 29. The fraction will not fit in the answer field, so you must convert it to a decimal and round to the appropriate number of places: $\frac{143}{29} = 4.93$.

12. B: The volume of a rectangular box can be determined using the formula $V = l \times w \times h$, where l is the length of the box, w is the width of the box, and h is the height of the box. Therefore, the volume of the box described in this question is equal to $5 \times 7 \times 9$, or 315 in^3.

13. C: Start by solving $5y - 20 < 0$ for y.

$$5y - 20 < 0$$
$$5y < 20$$
$$y < 4$$

Since y must be an integer, the answer must be 3 because 3 is the largest integer that is less than 4.

14. C: The total number of people mentioned is $20 + 13 = 33$, but there are only 25 cars. Therefore, $33 - 25 = 8$ cars must have both a man and a woman inside.

15. C: The line in the graph has a negative slope and a positive y-axis intercept, so the factor multiplying the variable x, or the slope, must be negative, and the constant, or y-intercept, must be positive. To find the slope, m, use the slope formula and the two points $(0,2)$ and $(3,-3)$.

$$m = \frac{y_2 - y_1}{x_2 - x_1} = \frac{-3 - 2}{3 - 0} = \frac{-5}{3}$$

Therefore, the slope of the line is $m = -\frac{5}{3}$. The y-intercept is the point where the line crosses the y-axis, which is $(0,2)$. Therefore, the value of b, the y-coordinate of the y-intercept, is 2. Substitute these values into the slope-intercept form of a line, $y = mx + b$.

$$y = -\frac{5}{3}x + 2$$

16. C: To solve this inequality, start by separating it into two inequalities because of the absolute value. $|x - 3|$ is equal to $x - 3$ or $-(x - 3)$.

$$5 < x - 3 < 7$$

$$5 + 3 < x - 3 + 3 < 7 + 3$$

$$8 < x < 10$$

$$5 < -(x - 3) < 7$$

$$-5 > x - 3 > -7$$

$$-5 + 3 > x - 3 + 3 > -7 + 3$$

$$-2 > x > -4$$

Since we know x is a negative integer, it must be –3 because of the inequality on the right. The absolute value of –3 is 3, so $|x| = 3$.

17. B: The total volume of the cylinder is given by $V = h\pi r^2 = 10\pi \times 1 = 31.4$, when $\pi = 3.14$. Since the slice is a straight, 60-degree slice, its volume is $\frac{1}{6}$ of this $\left(\frac{60}{360} = \frac{1}{6}\right)$, or 5.23.

18. B: The first function shifts the graph of $y = \frac{1}{x}$ to the left one unit and down three units. The domain and range of $y = \frac{1}{x}$ are $\{x: x \neq 0\}$ and $\{y: y \neq 0\}$, so the domain and range of $y = \frac{1}{x+1} - 3$ are $\{x: x \neq -1\}$ and $\{y: y \neq -3\}$. The element –3 is not in its range.

The second function shifts the graph of $y = \sqrt{x}$ to the right two units and down three units. The domain and range of $y = \sqrt{x}$ are $\{x: x \geq 0\}$ and $\{y: y \geq 0\}$, so the domain and range of

$y = \sqrt{x-2} - 3$ are $\{x: x \geq 2\}$ and $\{y: y \geq -3\}$. The domain contains the element 2, and the range contains the element –3.

The third function shifts the graph of $y = |x|$ to the left two units and down three units. The domain of $y = |x|$ is the set of all real numbers and the range is $\{y: y \geq 0\}$, so the domain of $y = |x-1| + 3$ is the set of all real numbers and the range is $\{y: y \geq 3\}$. The element –3 is not in its range.

The domain of the piecewise fourth function is the set of all real numbers, and the range is $\{y: y \geq 2\}$. The range does not contain the element –3.

19. C: If Q is divisible by both 7 and 2, it must be a multiple of 14, which is the least common multiple of both 2 and 7. Therefore, if one adds another multiple of 14 to Q, it will also be divisible by both 2 and 7. Of the choices given, only 28 is a multiple of 14.

20. D: Start by adding the number of blue and red fish together: $150 + 150 = 300$. This leaves only $400 - 300 = 100$ brown fish. Since the probability of pulling out any single fish is the same, he has a $\frac{100}{400} = \frac{1}{4} = 25\%$ chance of getting a brown fish.

21. A: Substitute the given values for a and b and then simplify using the order of operations.

$$\begin{aligned} a^2 + 3ab - b^2 &= (3)^2 + 3(3)(-2) - (-2)^2 \\ &= 9 + 3(3)(-2) - 4 \\ &= 9 - 18 - 4 \\ &= -13 \end{aligned}$$

Therefore, the value of the expression is –13.

22. C: Every possible combination of scores is a multiple of 7 since the two terms of the ratio have a sum of 7. Additionally, 16 is not divisible by 7, so it is not a possible total number of points the boys could have scored.

23. D: Recall that the general form of a quadratic expression is $ax^2 + bx + c$. A great way to factor quadratic expression like this, where $a = 1$ and all the answer choices are integer factors, would be to consider the factors of the last term, c. Specifically, any two factors of c that would add to b. Essentially: $f_1 \times f_2 = -12$ and $f_1 + f_2 = 1$. We can check the factors of –12.

f_1	f_2	$f_1 + f_2$
12	-1	11
6	-2	4
4	-3	1
3	-4	-1
2	-6	-4
1	-12	-11

The only option from this table that works is 4 and –3, which means the expression factors as $(x + 4)(x - 3)$.

24. C: The sentence in the question translates to $3x - 5 = 58$. This can be solved for x using normal algebra methods. Start by adding 5 to both sides of the equation.

$$3x = 63$$

Then, divide both sides by 3.

$$x = 21$$

25. A: A set of six numbers with an average of 4 must have a collective sum of 24 because $6 \times 4 = 24$. The two numbers that average 2 will add up to 4 ($2 \times 2 = 4$), so the remaining numbers must add up to 20 ($24 - 4 = 20$). The average of these four numbers can be calculated by dividing the sum by the amount of numbers: $20 \div 4 = 5$. Therefore, the average of the other four numbers is 5.

26. D: When asked to find the point of intersection of two lines, we are being asked to solve a system of equations. This system can be solved using the substitution method by substituting $x - 5$ for y in the first equation, $y = 2x + 3$.

$$x - 5 = 2x + 3$$

From here, solve for x.

$$-x - 5 = 3$$
$$-x = 8$$
$$x = -8$$

Now that the value of x is known, substitute this into either original equation and solve for y.

$$y = 2(-8) + 3 = -16 + 3 = -13$$

Therefore, the point of intersection for these two lines is $(-8, -13)$.

27. A: Start by substituting the function $f(x)$ into the expression $2f(x) - 3$.

$$2(2x^2 + 7) - 3$$

From here, simplify the expression using the distributive property.

$$4x^2 + 14 - 3$$

Finally, combine like terms.

$$4x^2 + 11$$

28. C: For this problem there are 3 inches in each segment, 12 inches in a foot, and 3 feet in a yard. Set up a conversion problem and simplify.

$$4.5\ \cancel{\text{yd}} \times \frac{3\ \cancel{\text{ft}}}{1\ \cancel{\text{yd}}} \times \frac{12\ \cancel{\text{in}}}{1\ \cancel{\text{ft}}} \times \frac{1\ \text{segment}}{\cancel{3\ \text{in}}} = 4.5 \times 12\ \text{segments} = 54\ \text{segments}$$

Therefore, a 4.5-yard line can be divided into 54 3-inch segments.

29. C: When the dress is marked down by 20%, the cost of the dress is 80% of its original price. Since a percentage can be written as a fraction by placing the percentage over 100, the reduced price of the dress can be written as $\frac{80}{100}x$, or $\frac{4}{5}x$, where x is the original price. When discounted an extra 25%, the dress costs 75% of the reduced price. This results in the expression $\frac{75}{100}\left(\frac{4}{5}x\right)$, which can be simplified to $\frac{3}{4}\left(\frac{4}{5}x\right)$, or $\frac{3}{5}x$. So the final price of the dress is three-fifths of the original price.

30. B: Dividing both sides of the equation by $\frac{1}{3}\pi h$ gives $r^2 = \frac{V}{\frac{1}{3}\pi h} = \frac{3V}{\pi h}$. We can then solve for r by taking the square root of both sides, which gives us $r = \sqrt{\frac{3V}{\pi h}}$.

31. A: The mean, or average, of the distribution can be computed by multiplying each grade by the number of students who obtained it, summing all the products, and then dividing by the total number of students. Here, $n = 4.2$. The median is the value where the number of students who received a lower grade is equal to the number of students who received a higher grade. Here, $p = 4$. The mode is the most frequently obtained grade, and here, $q = 3$. Thus, $n > p > q$.

32. D: Remember that when you multiply like bases, you add the exponents, and when you divide like bases, you subtract the exponents.

$$(xy)^{7y} - (xy)^y = (xy)^y[(xy)^{7y-y} - 1] = (xy)^y[(xy)^{6y} - 1]$$

33. B: If the averages are equal, then we have $\frac{x+y+z}{3} = \frac{a+b+c}{3}$, so it must be true that $(x + y + z) = (a + b + c)$. Therefore, the average of all six numbers is $\frac{(x+y+z)+(a+b+c)}{6} = \frac{2(x+y+z)}{6} = \frac{(x+y+z)}{3} = 23$.

34. 15: This system of equations can best be solved using the elimination method. Start by subtracting the second equation from the first.

$$\begin{array}{c} 2x + y + 7a = 50 \\ \underline{-(2x + y + 5a = 40)} \\ 2a = 10 \end{array}$$

This can then be solved for a by dividing both sides by 2.

$$a = 5$$

Substitute this value into either of the original equations and solve for $2x + y$.

$$\begin{aligned} 2x + y + 7(5) &= 50 \\ 2x + y + 35 &= 50 \\ 2x + y &= 15 \end{aligned}$$

35. B: $(6a)x^2$ is equivalent to $6 \times ax^2$, so ax^2 is $\frac{1}{6}$ of this, or $\frac{30}{6} = 5$.

36. A: Since a player cannot remove fewer than 1 or more than 3 toothpicks per turn, it follows that leaving 2, 3, or 4 toothpicks in a row allows a winning response, and that leaving 5 toothpicks forces the next player to leave 2, 3, or 4. Therefore, you should start by removing 1 toothpick.

37. A: Beginning by adding 7 to both sides of the inequality is an easier, more common, and recommended approach; however, dividing both sides by 3 is also mathematically correct because it produces an equivalent inequality and makes progress in isolating the variable. Dividing by 3, however, requires application of the distributive property on the left side to get the inequality $x - \frac{7}{3} < \frac{20}{3}$. This yields the solution $x < \frac{27}{3}$, which simplifies to $x < 9$.

38. D: The circular area covered by the sprinkler is πr^2, so the difference is obtained as $\pi(8)^2 - \pi(6)^2 = 64\pi - 36\pi = 28\pi = 28(3.14) = 87.92$. This rounds up to 88, so the area covered by the water increased by approximately 88 square feet.

39. C: Since the line is straight, the slope is the same throughout. Thus, if 5 y-units are traversed in going from $x = -3$ to $x = 0$ (where y increases from -5 to 0, to reach the origin), then 5 y-units will be traversed in going from $x = 0$ to $x = 3$.

40. A: The area of a triangle equals half the product of base times height. Since the base passes through the center, we have base $= 2r$ and height $= r$, so the area A is $A = \frac{r \times 2r}{2} = r^2$.

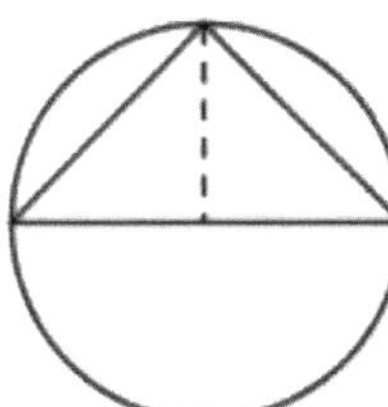

41. C: The probability of getting three aces in a row is the product of the probabilities for each draw. For the first ace, that is 4 in 52 since there are 4 aces in a deck of 52 cards. For the second, it is 3 in 51, since 3 aces and 51 cards remain; and for the third, it is 2 in 50. So, the overall probability, P, is $P = \frac{4}{52} \times \frac{3}{51} \times \frac{2}{50} = \frac{24}{132{,}600} = \frac{1}{5{,}525}$.

42. D: This answer is obtained by moving the second term to the right of the equality and changing its sign:

$$ax^2 + by = 0$$

$$ax^2 = -by$$

43. 1: At $y = 2$, we see that $x = 2$ for the plotted line. The equation for a straight line is of the form $y = mx + b$, where m is the slope of the line and b is the y-intercept. If the new line passes through the origin, then $b = 0$. Substitute the values for x, y, and b in the equation and solve for m.

$$2 = m(2) + 0$$
$$2 = 2m$$
$$1 = m$$

Therefore, the slope of the line that passes through the origin and the point (2,2) is 1.

44. D: It is certainly possible for two distinct quadratic functions to intersect at no points; one simple example is provided by the quadratic functions $y = x^2$ and $y = x^2 + 1$. For these to have an intersection there must be at least one solution to the equation $x^2 = x^2 + 1$, which implies $0 = 1$, which is clearly impossible. It is also possible for two quadratic functions to intersect in exactly one point, if that point is the vertex of both quadratic functions; take for instance the quadratic functions $y = x^2$ and $y = -x^2$, which intersect only at the origin, (0, 0). Two distinct quadratic functions intersecting at a point other than a mutual vertex will intersect at two points; an example is the quadratic functions $y = x^2$ and $y = -x^2 + 2$, which will intersect at the points (1,1) and $(-1,1)$.

45. D: The radius, R, of the satellite's orbit is the sum of Earth's radius plus the satellite's orbital altitude, or $R = 4{,}400$ mi. The circumference of the circular orbit is therefore $C = 2\pi r = 2\pi(4{,}400) = 8{,}800\pi$ mi. Since 40 minutes is one-third of the satellite's 120-minute orbital time, it traverses one-third of this distance in that time.

$$D = \frac{1}{3} \times 8{,}800(3.14) \approx 9{,}210.67$$

Therefore, the distance the satellite travels is approximately 9,211 miles.

46. D: The line in the graph has a constant value of y, one that does not change regardless of the value of x. This is a special case of the equation for the straight line, $y = mx + b$, for which $m = 0$.

47. D: Find the area of each figure. The area of a square is $A = s^2$, so the area of figure C is 7^2 or 49 in^2. The area of a circle can be determined by using the formula $A = \pi \times r^2$. Also, note that the radius of a circle is equal to half of the circle's diameter. This means that the radius of figure A is 4.5 inches, and the radius of figure B, which is stated within the question, is 5 inches. Therefore, the area of figure A is equal to 3.14×4.5^2 or 63.585 in^2, and the area of figure B is equal to 3.14×5^2 or 78.5 in^2. In order, $49\ \text{in}^2 < 63.585\ \text{in}^2 < 78.5\ \text{in}^2$, so $C < A < B$.

48. D: When no tickets are sold, $N = 0$. The following equation can be created and solved for p.

$$\begin{aligned} 0 &= 25{,}000 - 0.1p^2 \\ 0.1p^2 &= 25{,}000 \\ p^2 &= \frac{25{,}000}{0.1} \\ p^2 &= 250{,}000 \\ p &= 500 \end{aligned}$$

Therefore, the lowest price at which they will sell no tickets at all is \$500.

49. B: Remember that profit = (tickets sold) × (price) − cost. The number of tickets sold is given by the equation $N = 25000 - 0.1p^2$. Multiplying this expression by price, p, gives $25{,}000p - 0.1p^3$, and subtracting cost gives $Q = 25{,}000p - 0.1p^3 - 500{,}000$.

50. A: Rearranging the first equation gives $x^2 = 24 - y^2$. Now, substituting this value into the second equation gives $2(24 - y^2) + 3y^2 = 52 \Rightarrow 48 - 2y^2 + 3y^2 = 52$. Rearranging once again gives $y^2 = 4$, or $y = \pm 2$.

51. C: Equilateral triangles and regular hexagons may tessellate a plane. Each triangle may be attached to each side of a hexagon, leaving no gaps in the plane.

52. A: If the digits in a number add up to a multiple of 3, it is also divisible by 3. For instance, in the number 27, $2 + 7 = 9$, which is a multiple of 3.

53. D: Since Hannah spends at least \$16, the relation of the cost of a package of coffee to the minimum cost may be written as $4p \geq 16$. Alternatively, the inequality may be written as $16 \leq 4p$.

54. B: Since the events are mutually exclusive, the sum of their individual probabilities is 1.0. Subtracting 0.6 from 1.0 yields 0.4. Therefore, the correct choice is B.

55. C: The mean is the average of the data and can be found by dividing the sum of the data by the number of data: $\frac{16+18+20+21+34+45+49}{7} = 29$. The median is the middle data point when the data are ranked numerically. The median is 21.

Science

1. C: Of the sites listed, the phi value for site MD, 2.73 phi, is the largest value. The text explains how phi varies inversely with particle size, so these are the smallest particles.

2. A: According to the definition of phi supplied in the text, the range 1.0 to 4.0 phi units corresponds to particle sizes in the range 0.06 to 0.5 mm.

3. A: At all of the sites except site ND, the particle size distributions are tightly centered around a well-defined modal value. At site ND, the distribution is spread out over a broader range, and there is no well-defined central value.

4. D: Each unit of added phi value in the negative direction corresponds to a doubling of the particle size, so –1 corresponds to 2 mm, –2 to 4 mm, and –3 to 8 mm.

5. A: The curves represent the distance traveled, and they approximate a straight line. The slope of the line represents the speed of travel. Although the curve in part (b) has a negative slope, the absolute value of that slope will be a positive value, representing speed of transport towards the west.

6. B: The steepest slopes correspond to the greatest values of *mab*, or meters above bottom. These are the shallowest waters.

7. A: According to the passage, the giant cane toad is a large frog species that can be found in a variety of colors, including shades of brown. The poison dart frog is small and has bright colors. The conclusion is that poisonous frogs can be found in different sizes and colors. Since the passage mentions that the poison from the poison dart frog has been used by humans, it can be assumed that they are in areas where humans will encounter them, so choice B is incorrect. Choice C states that all poisonous frogs have bright colors, and while this is true of the poison dart frog, the giant cane toad does not have bright colors. The giant cane toad is very large, meaning choice D is incorrect since it states that poisonous frogs tend to be very small.

8. A: The poison dart frog has been used by humans who add the frogs' poison to the end of dart tips. The giant cane toad has been used by humans to eat the pests on sugarcane. There is no mention in the passage of either being endangered, and the giant cane toad's toxin will cause skin irritation, not death, in humans. They eat insects and arthropods, so they are not herbivores.

9. A: When the northern glass frog is described as nocturnal, this means that it is mainly active at night. The giant cane toad is also described as nocturnal, and the passage indicates that the giant cane toad is primarily active during the night. When an animal is active during the day and inactive at night, it is diurnal (choice B). An animal that is mostly active during twilight is crepuscular (choice C). *Cathemeral* describes a pattern of activity during both daylight and darkness (choice D).

10. C: Without the apex predators, their prey would experience a population explosion, which would then cause the prey to not have enough food to eat. The lack of apex predators would affect the ecosystem negatively.

11. B: According to the passage, any animal that feeds on zooplankton is a secondary consumer. A secondary consumer will be preyed upon by larger animals that are considered tertiary consumers. Zooplankton are considered a primary consumer.

12. C: The tension in the string is proportional to the mass of the hanging weight. According to the data in Table 2, as the mass of the hanging weight increases, so does the frequency of the wave. The two variables are therefore positively correlated. To select between the remaining choices, we have to check whether they are directly proportional. If they were, this would mean that when the tension in the string was multiplied by some factor, the frequency would be multiplied by the same factor. But this is not the case—when the mass of the hanging weight is doubled, from 500 g to 1,000 g, the frequency is increased only by a factor of about 1.4, from 63 Hz to 88 Hz. The two variables are therefore *not* directly proportional.

13. B: The pulley is there only to change the direction of the force applied by the hanging weight; there is no clear reason to expect that changing the radius of the pulley would have an interesting effect on the frequency of the standing waves. The frequency of the wave generator corresponding to the standing waves is what is being measured as the dependent variable; it can't also be the independent variable. Finally, the speed of the wave in the string is not a quantity that can straightforwardly be varied directly; it depends on other factors, such as the tension in the string (which the student already used as an independent variable) and the mass of the string (which could be an interesting independent variable to use but is not one of the choices). This leaves the correct answer, the length of the string, as another quantity the student might use as an independent variable.

14. A: It's important to keep track of units in calculations. One newton of force is equal to one kilogram times meter per second squared ($1\text{ N} = 1\text{ kg m/s}^2$); to find the force in newtons, then, the student should have multiplied the mass of the hanging weight in kilograms by the acceleration of gravity in meters per second squared. The correct tension is, therefore, $(0.500\text{ kg})(9.8\text{ m/s}^2) = 4.9\text{ N}$.

15. C: In Trial 9, the student found that a frequency of 79 Hz gave rise to two standing waves when the mass of the hanging weight was 800 g. Based on Study 1, it seems that for a given tension, the frequency is directly proportional to the number of waves. (The frequency for two waves is about double that for one, the frequency for three waves is about triple that for one, etc.) We would therefore expect that the frequency for four standing waves should be twice the frequency for two standing waves. In this case, that means that the frequency for four standing waves when the mass of the hanging weight is 800 g should be about 2×79 Hz, which is about 160 Hz.

16. B: When you plot a graph, the convention is to put the independent variable on the x-axis and the dependent variable on the y-axis. In this case, the student is varying the mass of the hanging weight and testing how this affects the frequency at which there are two standing waves. Therefore, the mass of the hanging weight is the independent variable (the quantity that the student is most directly varying), and so it goes on the x-axis.

17. D: There is no obvious reason to expect that the mass of the string should vary significantly between trials, nor that the surroundings of the experiment should be vibrating. The number of standing waves is an integer that should be straightforward to count. The largest source of error is likely to be the uncertainty in finding the exact frequency corresponding to a specific number of standing waves; it may be difficult to tell if the wave driver is at exactly the correct frequency to produce standing waves or if the waves might be moving slightly and the frequency might be slightly off.

18. A: To improve the validity of the design of this experiment, Malik should use three of the same type of plant. Since the three plants used in the experiment have different growth patterns and nutritional needs, the variation in plant types is a confounding factor that will lead to unreliable results. Using the same plant types will minimize the effect that the inherent plant differences have on the results.

19. D: To improve the design of the experiment, and to provide a baseline for the results, Malik should add a control group to the experiment. In this case, he should use the same type of plant for each liquid tested, along with a fourth plant that receives only plain tap water. This would determine a baseline of the expected growth of the plant without the addition of other types of liquid, and the growth of the other plants could be compared to this baseline to determine the effects of the other liquids.

20. A: To find the probability of both plants sprouting, multiply the probabilities of each event occurring. First convert the percentages to decimals: 50% = 0.50 and 70% = 0.70. Then, multiply the decimals and convert back to a percentage: $0.50 \times 0.70 = 0.35$, or 35%. The probability that both plant species sprout within the first 14 days after planting the seeds is 35%.

21. D: To find the probability that neither of the plants will sprout within the first 14 days, first find the probability that each individual plant will not sprout. Convert the probabilities of the plants spouting from percentages to decimals, then subtract this number from 1 to get the decimal probability that the plant will not sprout. For plant A, this is $1 - 0.50 = 0.50$. For plant B, it is $1 - 0.70 = 0.30$. Next, multiply these probabilities together and convert back to a percentage: $0.50 \times 0.30 = 0.15$, or 15%.

22. B: Jaden did not form a hypothesis before proceeding with his experiment. The hypothesis is an assumption that can be tested to see if it is true. A hypothesis for this scenario could be, "If the plants receive more sunlight, they will grow taller due to photosynthesis." Jaden performed data collection when he recorded plant growth. He researched when he investigated the link between plant growth and sunlight. He set up an experiment with the scenario of two groups of plants, one in full sun and one in the shade.

23. D: In Jaden's experiment, sunlight positively affects the growth of milkweed. His experiment did not involve other types of plants, so it does not lead to a conclusion about all plants. Since he had researched how plants produce energy through photosynthesis, which fuels a plant's cellular growth, it would not be a reasonable conclusion that photosynthesis does not affect plant growth.

24. B: Since both mass and proximity positively affect gravitational pull, the Moon having a larger mass would likely result in more-extreme tides due to a higher gravitational pull. The Earth would still experience high tides, and the Sun would still affect the tidal pattern.

25. C: Gravitational pull is a force of attraction that draws two objects toward one another. The force of attraction is related to the masses of the objects, so larger masses have stronger gravitational pull than smaller masses do. Proximity plays a role, too, so objects that are closer together have a stronger gravitational pull than objects further apart do.

26. A: The passage states that extra-high tides and extra-low tides occur when the Earth, Moon, and Sun align. It also states that the highest tides, called spring tides, occur twice a month. These spring tides are caused by the alignment of these three celestial bodies. The Sun exerts a lower gravitational pull on Earth than the Moon does, so the Moon causes higher tides than the Sun does. The side of Earth that is facing the Moon is not always the same, so each location on Earth experiences high and low tides from the pull of the Moon. Spring tides are the highest tides, while neap tides are lower tides.

27. B: It takes 8.5 minutes for light to travel 1 AU of distance and Saturn is 9.58 AU from the Sun. Set up the proportion $\frac{8.5 \text{ minutes}}{1 \text{ AU}} = \frac{x}{9.58 \text{ AU}}$, and solve for x.

$$x \times 1 \text{ AU} = 8.5 \text{ minutes } \times 9.58 \text{ AU} = 81.43 \text{ minutes}$$

$$\frac{81.43 \text{ minutes}}{60 \text{ minutes/hour}} = 1.36 \text{ hours}$$

28. C: Given that the time for light to travel to the asteroid is 7.2 minutes, and it takes 8.5 minutes for light to travel 1 AU of distance, set up the proportion $\frac{7.2 \text{ minutes}}{x} = \frac{8.5 \text{ minutes}}{1 \text{ AU}}$ and then solve for x.

$$7.2 \text{ minutes} \times 1 \text{ AU} = 8.5 \text{ minutes } \times x$$

$$7.2 \text{ AU} = 8.5x$$

$$x = \frac{7.2}{8.5} = 0.847 \text{ AU}$$

An asteroid that is 0.847 AU away from the Sun is between Venus and Earth.

29. D: The correct sequence of components used during respiration starts with the nose and mouth, which bring air into the body. Next, the air passes through the larynx and moves on through the trachea. The trachea brings the air to the bronchioles, which have alveoli at the ends of them.

30. B: Internal respiration involves the processes that take place at a cellular level. During internal respiration, the red blood cells use oxygen and then transport waste back to the lungs. The larynx, trachea, and bronchioles are all components of external respiration.

31. A: During respiration, gas is exchanged within the lungs by alveoli, and the alveoli then move carbon dioxide from the bloodstream so it can be exhaled. Oxygen is taken into the bloodstream by the alveoli, which are the tiny air sacs at the ends of the bronchioles. The pharynx is a part of the respiratory system that is used to carry air to the larynx.

32. B: The pulmonary artery brings blood away from the heart and into the alveoli, where internal respiration takes place. The pulmonary vein then takes the blood back away from the alveoli to the heart. The bronchioles are the airways that lead to the alveoli.

33. D: At the left end of the curve, the solution has a low pH of less than 7, which means that it is acidic. This represents the solution when no titrant has been added yet, which means it represents the pH of the titrand. The titrand is therefore acidic. As more titrant is added, the pH increases, eventually rising past the neutral pH of 7 and becoming basic. If adding the titrant to the acidic titrand makes the solution basic, then the titrant must be basic.

34. C: The graph of the titration curve consistently rises to the right, which means that the pH consistently increases as more titrant is added. However, we're not asked whether the pH is increasing or decreasing—we're asked about the rate of increase. The rate of increase is represented by the slope (steepness) of the graph—the closer the graph is to horizontal, the lower the rate of increase, and the closer it is to vertical, the higher the rate of increase. The graph starts out close to horizontal, with a low rate of increase and then gradually gets steeper and steeper until about 30 mL of titrant have been added. During this interval, therefore, the rate of increase is rising. To the right of this point, however, the graph then flattens out again, becoming once again close to horizontal—the rate of increase is falling. So, the rate of increase first rises (between 0 mL and 30 mL on the x-axis) and then falls (between 30 mL and 60 mL).

35. A: If the titrand is more highly concentrated, we would expect to have to add more titrant to neutralize it. This means that the values on the x-axis corresponding to different parts of the graph would be larger. The first choice is the only graph that depicts this. (Note, for instance, that the steepest part of the graph corresponds in this graph to 50 mL of titrant added, as opposed to 30 mL in the original graph.) The second choice shows the opposite, with smaller quantities of titrant yielding the same results. In the last two choices, the scale of the x-axis and the quantities of titrant added are unchanged, but the graph is moved vertically; the pH of the point of steepest descent is changed. There is no obvious reason to expect that this should happen. (We could expect that with a more highly concentrated titrand the initial solution might be more acidic—but this is in fact shown in the correct choice, where the initial pH is lower than in the original titration curve.)

36. D: There is no obvious reason why the student should favor indicators of particular colors; what is important for the experiment is the pH range of the indicator's color change. Ideally, the student should want the color change to occur over as small a range of titrant added as possible so that the pH range can be matched to a specific amount of titrant added, or at least a relatively narrow range of titrant added. This means the student should choose an indicator that changes color at a pH range corresponding to the steepest part of the titration curve. The steepest part of the titration curve is at a pH of between 8.5 and 9.5, so the best indicator to choose is phenolphthalein, which changes color over a pH range of about 8.3 to 10.0.

37. A: As more of the titrant is added to the titrand, the pH of this mixture changes. It is the pH of this mixture that we are measuring, so this is where the indicator should be added. The pH of the titrant does not change; there is no reason to add the indicator there. Because we are using the indicator to detect the change in the pH during the titration, the indicator certainly must be present for the titration, and it doesn't make sense to add it afterward.

38. C: A hypothesis should include the relevant variables and the predicted outcome. The hypothesis in choice C includes both the variables and the predicted outcome. Once Joe conducts the experiment, he can find out if the outcome of the experiment matches his hypothesis. Hypotheses should not include opinions.

39. B: When Joe places the cold-stratified seeds and the regular seeds in windows that face different directions, they receive different amounts of sunlight, which can affect the experiment. To create a more valid experiment, Joe would need to expose the seeds to the same amounts of sunlight. With this variation, it will be difficult to know whether the sunlight or the cold stratification made the plants germinate more readily.

40. A: The independent variable is the variable that is manipulated by the person performing the experiment. In this case, Joe is cold stratifying one set of seeds, and not cold stratifying the other set, to see how it affects germination. The dependent variable is what is being tested in the experiment. In this case, the germination rate is being tested. The amount of water and soil type are kept the same for each set, and the room temperature is kept the same as well.

41. B: If Joe measures the amount of water used, he can apply the same amount of water to each set of seeds and keep the watering consistent. Recording the plant growth weekly instead of daily would not strengthen the experiment. Using a different type of soil for each set of seeds would introduce a new variable, and using a smaller sample size would weaken the experiment.

42. D: Cold stratification is a process that involves exposing seeds to moist, cold conditions to encourage germination. This process happens in nature when seeds fall to the ground and are exposed to winter weather and wet conditions before they germinate in the spring. The process can be simulated with a refrigerator and damp materials, such as paper towels, and some seeds germinate better when they are cold stratified.

43. A: The data table clearly shows that the final temperature rises as the initial temperature of the metal sample rises. (Even without seeing the data table, this is what we would expect; the higher the initial temperature of the metal sample, the more thermal energy it contains to release into the water, and the higher the final temperature of the system.) Note that the correct graph depicts a linear relationship between the two quantities, whereas the incorrect graph depicts a markedly nonlinear relationship in which the final temperature rises rapidly at first but then levels off for larger initial temperatures. Examining the data table, we see that there is no such leveling off; the rate of increase remains more or less constant. Between the first two data points, for instance, the rate of increase is $\frac{21.5\text{ °C}-21.1\text{ °C}}{100\text{ °C}-80\text{ °C}} = \frac{0.4\text{ °C}}{20\text{ °C}} = 0.02$, whereas between the last two data points the rate of increase is $\frac{23.3\text{ °C}-22.5\text{ °C}}{200\text{ °C}-160\text{ °C}} = \frac{0.8\text{ °C}}{40\text{ °C}} = 0.02$—the same value. The relationship therefore appears to be linear, matching the graph in the first choice.

44. D: The units that the student uses to measure the temperature should not affect the general trend of the results—the numbers may be different, but the shape of the graph should not change. Because the temperature is on the y-axis of the graph, it is the y-axis that will be labeled differently if the temperature is measured in different units.

45. A: Most experimental measurements have unavoidable random error; due to slight variations in the equipment or surroundings or limitations in measurement, the results may vary. The variation due to random error is equally likely to give results higher or lower than the theoretical value. When you take multiple measurements and average the results, the random error tends to cancel out, and its effects are reduced.

Systematic error is a form of error that can be caused by flaws in the equipment or methodology that causes all the measurements to be off in the same direction and by about the same amount. Because systematic error is consistent in different trials, multiple trials will not reduce systematic error; it must be recognized and accounted for in other ways.

There is no meaningful sense in which the system described should "accommodate" and no reason to expect that later trials should be more accurate than earlier ones.

46. C: Trial 4 and trial 7 both involve a metal sample with a mass of 400 g and an initial temperature of 160 °C. All the other choices are pairs of trials that differ either in the mass of the metal sample or its initial temperature or both.

47. B: The purpose of the insulated container is to prevent, or at least minimize, heat exchange with the surrounding environment outside the system so that all but a negligible amount of the heat lost by the metal sample goes toward heating up the water. If the container was not insulated, then heat exchange would also occur with the surroundings until the system and its surroundings reached the same temperature. The system would certainly not reach a final temperature lower than its surroundings as that would violate the second law of thermodynamics.

48. A: According to the passage, specific heat is a measurement of the amount of heat necessary to raise the temperature of a substance by a particular amount. If saltwater has a lower specific heat than pure water, then it takes less heat to raise its temperature by the same amount—or, equivalently, the same amount of heat will cause a larger rise in temperature. Therefore, as heat flows from the metal into the saltwater, the temperature of the saltwater will rise at a faster rate than that of the pure water, and the mixture will stabilize at a higher temperature.

49. C: The chart shows that the combination of A and O results in A, and the combination of O and O results in O. If a child receives an O and a B allele, the result will be type B blood. There are only four possible phenotypes total, so they must all be A, B, O, or AB.

50. D: According to the chart, when a child receives an A allele and an O allele, the result is type A blood. This is also true for a B allele combined with an O allele. Because of this, the conclusion can be made that the A and B alleles are dominant over the O allele.

51. D: If the duration of the experiment was increased from 7 weeks to 20 weeks, the scientist would have the opportunity to see if the plants went through multiple growth spikes during that time or if they mainly happened during the first 7 weeks. Increasing the cost would not be a benefit of the increase in duration. Increasing the possibility of error would not be a benefit either. While finding the optimal temperature might take time, it is not being altered in the experiment.

52. C: Since the cuttings have been planted in the same soil and have been kept in a room with a constant temperature exposed to the same lighting, the best way to increase the reliability of the data would be to increase the sample size. Increasing the sample size will reduce the impact of any individual variations. The scientist is already checking the growth at regular weekly intervals, as shown in the chart.

53. D: Using the data in the chart, the median of the numbers is found by placing the data for plant growth in order and finding the number in the middle. The middle number is 1.9. To take the mean, or average, of the data, add the numbers to get a total of 18.4, then divide by 7 to get 2.6. The mode is the number that appears the most, and none of the data repeats. Due to the outliers in the data, the best measure of central tendency to predict plant growth in this case is the median.

54. B: The passage states that the increase in carbon dioxide has been trapping extra heat near the Earth's surface and causing the temperature to slowly rise. The human cause of this is an increase in the burning of fuels, such as natural gas, coal, and oil. This releases more CO_2 into the atmosphere. The other answer choices describe human activities that contribute to global warming through the release of methane (A), chlorofluorocarbons (C), and nitrous oxide (D).

55. D: Chlorofluorocarbons, or CFCs, come from an industrial origin and do not exist in nature. They are refrigerants, spray can propellants, and solvents. Carbon dioxide, CO_2, comes from the exhalation of animals and the burning of fossil fuels. Methane, CH_4, can come from the breakdown of plant matter and the emissions of livestock. Nitrous oxide, N_2O, can come from the burning of vegetation and fossil fuels, but it also arises from soil in natural ecosystems.

56. A: The passage states that the increase in carbon dioxide can be partially attributed to the burning of gas, coal, and oil. If humans can find alternative forms of energy, it is reasonable to believe that their contributions to global warming can be changed. The temperature of the Earth will likely not fall soon due to the ongoing increases in greenhouse gases. Farming and raising animals are both creating greenhouse gases, just in different ways. CFCs were found to be dangerous, and alternatives are now being used, so they have been phased out. There is no evidence in the passage that they are safe in any amount.

57. C: According to the information given, the genotypes SS and Ss will both result in red spots. Since there are 33 ladybugs with the SS genotype and 38 with the Ss genotype out of 100, add 33 to 38 to get 71. To get the percentage, divide 71 by the total number of ladybugs (100) to get 0.71, then multiply that by 100 to get the percentage: 0.71 times 100 is 71%.

58. D: The graph provided shows that the line for the flower growth data starts just above 20 cm at a pH of 5.8 and rises to 38 cm at a pH of approximately 6.2. Flower growth reaches 40 cm at a pH of approximately 6.4. The line then rises rapidly, reaching a maximum of 57 cm at a pH of approximately 6.6. It drops slowly until a pH of approximately 6.8, and then quickly drops to 28 cm before the graph ends at a pH of 7. This aligns most closely with the flower growth data set shown in Choice D. The data for the pH values and flower growth are reversed in Choice A. In Choice B, the values for the flower growth data are too high and do not align with the graph. In Choice C, the pH values are too high and do not align with the graph.

59. B: The independent variable in this case is the amount of fertilizer being used. An independent variable is one that the person or people conducting the experiment manipulate to find out what effect it has on something else; the something else, which in this case is plant growth, is called the dependent variable. In this case, John and his friends are changing or manipulating the amount of fertilizer used to find out its effect on the plants. The number of people conducting the experiment is not something they are changing or manipulating. The temperature of the air in the greenhouse, as well as the weather outside of the greenhouse, are also not being manipulated to conduct the experiment.

60. B: When research shows contradictory findings, the best approach is to analyze the sample sizes, methodologies, and study findings to look for the factors that affected those outcomes. A small sample size can lead to a less-reliable result. Different research designs and different participant demographics can lead to different results. Choice A is incorrect because disregarding this research does not take into consideration the insights it might offer. Choice C is incorrect because all of the research must be considered, not only the parts that support a predetermined conclusion. Choice D is similarly incorrect because it disregards a study that does not support the predetermined conclusion.

Social Studies

1. B: When President Kennedy described outer space as having no strife, no prejudice, and no national conflict, he painted it as a beckoning, or appealing, destination that is free from these negative characteristics. Kennedy described space in a positive light while attempting to invoke the pioneering attitudes of the American people.

2. C: The use of repetition in Kennedy's speech served to highlight the urgency and importance in his message. Kennedy stated, "We choose to go to the moon. We choose to go to the moon in this decade and do the other things, not because they are easy, but because they are hard, because that goal will serve to organize and measure the best of our energies and skills, because that challenge is one that we are willing to accept..." This repetition was used to implore the audience to consider the importance of space travel for Americans.

3. B: Kennedy used loaded language within his speech to appeal to the emotions of the audience and persuade the audience toward his point of view. Loaded language is an appeal to emotions, using words with strong positive or negative connotations, in contrast with an appeal to logic. In this example, Kennedy used deeply emotional language to convince the audience that it was their duty as a country to support the moon mission.

4. D: According to the chart, when demand for the coffee is increased (D1 to D2), price will also increase (P1 to P2). This can be seen easily where the D1 and D2 lines intersect with the S line.

5. C: Exchanging existing equipment for more-efficient equipment would allow more coffee to be ground and supplied to the market with little to no cost increase. Expanding to a second manufacturing facility would increase supply but would likely increase cost as well. Hiring several new employees would not increase supply. Switching to a certified organic supplier would increase cost but not affect supply.

6. C: The larger map of Canada shows that this small area of Ontario is further south than most of the country, so it has a warmer climate than most of the country. The area includes the large and populous cities Toronto and Hamilton and their suburbs. It does have multiple lakes, but it is far away from much of the northern and western regions of Canada. Expansion is limited by the lakes on either side and the neighboring US state of New York.

7. B: The cities marked on the first map of Canada are mostly located near oceans, lakes, or rivers. Cities are commonly located near water for ease of travel and trade. The marked cities are fairly evenly distributed throughout the eastern and western sides of the country and are not close to each other. There are more cities in the southern area, due to the colder climate of the northern parts of Canada, but there are many in the northern areas as well. Some of the cities are located along the border with the US, but many are not.

8. B: In this speech, President Wilson asked Congress to consider Germany's action as an act of war and to take defensive action. Throughout the speech, Wilson described the objectives of the US as to protect peace and justice. He characterized Germany as a menace and said that it was the end to the United States' neutrality in the war.

9. A: In this excerpt, the *New York Times* article gave a biased account of Wilson's speech, emphasizing the applause and cheers he received when delivering the message to Congress. By leading with the line that the "audience that cheered him as he has never been cheered in the Capitol in his life," the article set up the speech as an overwhelmingly positive interaction with Congress. An objective account would present the facts without bias. If the excerpt was symbolic, it would use words to symbolize specific concepts or events. An analytical account would interpret the facts of the situation.

10. C: President Wilson's speech used loaded language to persuade Congress that there was no other option than to declare war on Germany. Germany was described as a selfish and autocratic power, while the US was described as free and self-governed. Wilson referred multiple times to Germany as threatening peace. The *New York Times* article described Wilson's speech in a wholly positive light, focusing on the applause and acceptance he gained from Congress, and again invoking the threat to peace in the world. The article was meant to persuade the American people that Wilson's declaration was rightful and unavoidable.

11. A: This political cartoon portrays women who oppose their own right to vote as on the same side as child-labor employers and sweatshop owners. The nefarious expressions of the male chorus characterize them as bad people, and the political boss conductor is leading them all as a group. The caption also emphasizes that the male chorus of poor labor practices supports the female soloist who does not vote. Therefore, it can be concluded that the artist believes, unlike the people in the cartoon, that women should be allowed to vote.

12. D: According to the cartoon, as long as women are not voting, they are in accord with the poor labor practices. The men representing the labor leaders are happy that the woman is unable to vote.

If women were allowed to vote, it would impact the labor bosses negatively because women would be able to vote against poor labor practices.

13. C: The data for the two categories in the chart show a mostly positive correlation. A positive correlation is when two variables increase or decrease together. In this case, the number of digital video game users has generally increased, aside from a small decrease from 2021 to 2022, and the number of music streaming subscribers has increased steadily in the years shown in the chart. There is no reason to think that the number of video game users caused the number of music streaming subscribers to change or that the number of music streaming subscribers caused the number of video game users to change.

14. B: To calculate the mean, or average, of this data set, add the numbers together to get 1,917 million (which is 1.917 billion):

$$198.6 + 229.5 + 304.9 + 341 + 400 + 443 = 1{,}917$$

Then, divide by 6, which is the number of items in the data set.

$$1{,}917 \div 6 = 319.5$$

The mean is 319.5 million. The median for this data set is 322.95 million, which is the average of the two middle numbers when the numbers in the data set are ordered from smallest to largest:

$$(304.9 + 341) \div 2 = 322.95$$

The values for mean and median are very close to one another, so they are both good measures of central tendency for this data set. Mode is the number that occurs the most often in a data set. There is no number in the data set that repeats, so this data set has no mode.

15. C: Causation is when one action causes another action. In this case, prohibiting the manufacture, sale, or transportation of alcohol caused organized crime to increase. Criminals did not bootleg alcohol because of an increase in the crime rate, but rather bootlegging was a factor contributing to the increase in crime. The sale of alcohol being banned and the use of liquor being prohibited both describe parts of Prohibition, not a causal relationship. People who drank in speakeasies were secretly accessing alcohol, but this is not a causal relationship.

16. D: Because the crime rate increased in response to the passage of the 18th Amendment and the prohibition of alcohol, once the 21st Amendment repealed the 18th Amendment, it is likely that the crime rate decreased again. Crime syndicates would no longer have a need to trade in illegal alcohol once it was available to the public again.

17. A: In 1933, the 21st Amendment repealed the 18th Amendment. The passage states that Prohibition, which was instituted by the 18th Amendment, lasted until 1933. It was at this time that the 21st Amendment revoked the 18th Amendment so that the sale, production, and transport of alcohol was no longer prohibited.

18. A: According to Article V, each state had one vote in Congress on issues affecting the United States. This means that a more populated state like Virginia, which in 1790 had a population of 747,000 people, and a less populated state like Delaware, which had a population of about 59,000 people, had the same amount of power despite the population disparity. The same situation exists today, as all states have two senators no matter what their populations are. The article states that no delegate would receive compensation for their term, and no state would be represented by less than two members. Freedom of speech could not be stifled within Congress.

19. D: According to this excerpt of Article VI, the responsibility of having a well-regulated militia ready at all times fell to the states rather than the federal government. Due to this lack of federal armed forces, the federal government could have a difficult time defending itself.

20. C: If a delegate of Congress is recalled, they are removed from office. Article V states that the delegates can be recalled by their states at any time within the year, and someone else can be sent in their place. If a delegate is recalled, or removed from office, the state would be able to substitute a different delegate instead.

21. B: In his speech, President Roosevelt stated that the US was "suddenly and deliberately attacked," alluding to the surprise nature of the attack. The announcement from Japan described the incident as "historic surprise attacks on Pearl Harbor." The President's speech did not characterize Japan's military as victorious, while the announcement described Japan's military as landing a "splendid" strike in which the US fleet "met with sudden defeat." The announcement described the attack's effect on England and portrayed the Philippines as an enemy.

22. C: President Roosevelt's address to Congress stated that the Japanese Ambassador delivered a formal reply to the US one hour after the bombing had commenced. This sentence does not contain opinions. The sentence from the Japanese announcement describing the two countries as headstrong used opinionated descriptions of both the countries and their future paths. The sentence describing the Imperial Forces' action included a description of a "splendid" strike, which is an opinion. The prediction of Singapore vanishing into nothing was an unverifiable prediction, and the description of the chapter in history as "glorious" was an opinion.

23. D: President Roosevelt's address described the US as at peace with Japan and described the attack as a "day which will live in infamy" since it was such a major event. The president described the attack as deliberate and goes on to allude that the threat will lead to conflict since there is no hope in continued diplomatic talks. The announcement to Japan described the attack as premeditated, deliberate, and a "historic surprise attack." It also described the attack as leading to a decisive victory, saying, "What these two headstrong countries are striving for will only lead them on a downhill path to military defeat."

24. B: In an inverse correlation, also called a negative correlation, the two variables move in opposite directions. This is evident throughout most of the chart, as the unemployment rate went down until 2019, while the inflation rate mostly rose. In 2020, the unemployment rate rose sharply, and the inflation rate went down. Then, in 2021-2022, the two rates moved in opposite directions again as the unemployment rate dropped and the inflation rate rose.

25. C: In this research, the economist is looking for causes of changes to the inflation rate. The inflation rate is the dependent variable. The independent variable is the unemployment rate, which potentially causes the inflation rate to change. The economist could check other independent variables, such as the exchange rate, to see their impact on and relationship with changes in the inflation rate.

26. B: Black Americans began to leave the city in large numbers in about 1970, after Martin Luther King Jr. was assassinated in 1968 and the city suffered significant damage in the riots that followed. Until then, the population of black Americans had steadily increased throughout the city's history.

27. B: According to the article, Nixon was slow in recognizing the impact of the Kent State shooting, in which anti-war protestors were killed, and did not censure the Guardsmen involved. His response was feeble, and it lowered morale at home. The author used strong language to condemn the shooting and stated that Nixon's response to the shooting was slow and consisted only of an obvious comment. The author characterized Nixon's judgment as "dangerously wrong" in assessing the risk in the response at home, which implies that his judgement in the war itself may also be disastrously wrong. These factors led the author to have an unfavorable view of the war effort.

28. C: This statement simply reports that four students were gunned down at Kent State. The other choices include opinionated and loaded language. The author characterized Nixon's recognition of the Kent State shootings' impact as "sadly slow," called the administration an "artful, managerial mechanism," and described Nixon as "dangerously wrong" in his assessment of the risk involved in the response at home.

29. D: The author's characterization of Nixon's unfulfilled promise to the nation as "mocked" shows that the author does not hold Nixon's word in high regard. The article overall projects an negative opinion of how Nixon handled public protests, and this biased line reinforces the author's opinion.

30. A: Bills are given a code that corresponds to the house of Congress where it originated. A bill starting with the code H.R. originated in the House of Representatives. Once the bill is introduced, it is then referred to a committee within that house. The committee will analyze the bill and could revise it prior to the next step.

31. C: The checks and balances built into the process of turning a bill into a law involve each branch of government making sure that the other branches do not have too much power. In this case, the legislative branch, which is made up of the Senate and the House of Representatives, is balanced by the power of the executive branch, which includes the president. If the legislative branch approves a law, the president can still veto it if he disagrees with it.

32. D: In this passage, the word *override* is used to describe what Congress can do to counteract the president's veto. If Congress still passes a bill through a majority vote after the president's veto, they are using their authority to reject the president's decision. If the president lets a bill sit for 10 days and Congress adjourns during that time, the bill will not pass and Congress cannot override the bill's failure. In other words, they are not able to use their authority to reject the president's decision to not approve the bill.

33. B: This speech, which was part of a series, was meant as propaganda to help raise money, in the form of Liberty Loans, to fund the war. The speaker talks of a spy watching the audience, and describes what they should do to appear as a united and strong country in the face of the enemy: lend more money to the government so as to outspend and defeat the Germans.

34. C: By describing the four freedoms and explaining how they should be extended to the rest of the world, Roosevelt positioned the US to join the fight against tyranny and not only protect their freedoms but also attempt to spread freedom to other countries. He ended the speech with "there can be no end save victory," referring to the struggle to gain or keep those fundamental rights.

35. C: According to the graph, when less than 70% of the population (70 out of 100 people) has internet access, the GDP is not significantly affected by internet usage. When between 70% and 90% of the population has internet access, GDP grows rapidly along with internet usage. When internet usage is above 90%, the graph of the GDP becomes almost entirely horizontal, which means that there is growth in GDP that is not related to internet usage.

36. C: Article II Section 1 of the Constitution states that in case of a president leaving office, the powers and duties of the office of president will devolve on, or be transferred to, the vice president. Section 1 of the 25th Amendment also says that if the president leaves office, the vice president will become president.

37. D: An emolument is some form of payment, such as a salary or fee. Article II states that the president's compensation, or pay, for serving as president is a fixed amount that cannot be changed during the presidency and that the president may not "receive any other Emolument." This means that the salary is a form of emolument, and the only one that the president is allowed to receive.

38. A: These sections of the 25th Amendment establish what happens if a president or vice president cannot or will not perform their duties any longer. In the case of the president's death or resignation, the vice president will become president. If the vice president needs to be replaced, the president will nominate a replacement.

39. C: The main purpose of the Preliminary Emancipation Proclamation was to free slaves in states, or parts of states, that were part of the rebellion against the United States if those states did not end their rebellion. President Lincoln used this proclamation to clearly lay out his command that slavery would end in any state still part of the rebellion as of January 1, 1863. On that day, his Emancipation Proclamation did grant freedom to the slaves in those states and parts of states.

40. D: When the Emancipation Proclamation ordered slaves to be freed from any state that was part of the rebellion, it removed resources from those states. The rebel states used slaves to repair uniforms, prepare foods, build fortifications, and much more. Without this extra labor, the rebelling states lost these resources and soon lost the war.

41. B: President Lincoln stated that as of January 1, 1863, 100 days after the Preliminary Emancipation Proclamation was issued, the slaves would be freed in any state, or part of a state, that was part of the rebellion. By allowing 100 days for the proclamation to take effect, President Lincoln gave the rebelling states time to end their rebellion and keep slavery. If the states continued their rebellion against the United States, they would lose their slaves.

42. A: The nuclear arms race had recently begun, and the US had already used atomic bombs. Eisenhower first acknowledged the dangers and fears associated with the use of nuclear weapons since the widespread damage had already been seen. He then assured the UN General Assembly that the US could work toward using nuclear powers for good, positioning nuclear power as a force that could potentially help the US.

43. C: When aet contains skewed data, the mean (average) is not a good measure of central tendency. In this case, two candidates have significantly higher total spending than the other candidates, so the average will be much higher than what most candidates spend. Because the mean does not accurately represent spending for a typical candidate, it is not a useful number for understanding campaign spending in general.

44. D: This is a propaganda poster used during World War I, and it was meant to encourage people to buy government bonds to support the war effort. In the image, the young man is going off to join the war effort through the military. Since the older man is not going to fight, he is encouraged to also support the war effort, but in a different way—by buying government bonds through the Third Liberty Loan program.

45. B: Choice B contains the fact that King was arrested on a charge of parading without a permit. The other options include opinions. King characterized methods used in Alabama as "devious." He claimed that segregation "distorts the soul and damages the personality," which was his opinion. When he explained that "one who breaks an unjust law must do so openly, lovingly, and with a willingness to accept the penalty," he was expressing his opinion.

46. A: A positive correlation occurs when two variables move in the same direction. In this case, the chart shows that when the inflation rate goes down, the nominal interest rate goes down, and vice versa. A positive correlation does not mean that changes in one variable cause changes in the other, but it can indicate that there is a close relationship between the two variables.

47. D: When inflation is high, money has less purchasing power than when inflation is low. The Federal Reserve can raise the nominal interest rate to reduce borrowing and spending, and thus help dampen the effects of inflation. Inflation control is one of the primary reasons that the Federal Reserve changes the interest rates. This helps to control the stability and health of the overall economy.

48. D: Both accounts mention leaving Fort Clatsop on their return journey. The accounts were written on March 23, 1806, which Joseph Whitehouse noted was the day they left Fort Clatsop. Since the expedition began in Camp Wood, Fort Clatsop was their turnaround point, and from here they returned through the location marked as Nez Perce. This is where the expedition encountered a Native American tribe called the Nez Perce.

49. B: As a leader of the expedition, Clark documented his concern about the safety of the team leaving on the morning of March 23rd, 1806. He noted that the morning was so "raney and uncertain" that they were not sure whether it was a good time to leave for their journey back. The decision to leave during bad weather could impact the expedition and the safety of the men, so it was natural for Clark to express concern over the inclement weather and initial indecision.

50. A: Since Clark and Whitehouse documented the day with many similar details, the journal entries corroborate each other, and it is likely that they are reliable accounts of the day. Although Clark and Whitehouse had different positions and different perspectives, they often described events in a similar way, which strengthens the reliability of each account.

51. D: During the expedition, Lewis and Clark met and traded with Native Americans, including the Chinook tribe described in the journal entries. This trade and diplomacy benefited the United States, as the people were natives of the newly acquired territory and good relations with them would benefit the nation. There was no mention that elk was a new discovery, although they did eat elk on the expedition. The journey did not reach into the Spanish Territory, as shown on the map. The ability to travel in inclement weather was not new.

52. B: Tetsuzo wrote the letter from inside the camp, where he was one of the people who was interned after Roosevelt's executive order. He described the poor conditions in detail as someone experiencing it firsthand. The author of the newspaper article wrote about the situation as an outsider not experiencing the situation firsthand. The author praised the camp's living conditions without being personally impacted by them.

53. A: The civil rights protests drew attention to the issue of voting rights after the deadly incident in Selma, AL. This incident drew the attention of people across the US, including President Johnson. Because of the attention on this issue and the negative ramifications of unfair voting rights, President Johnson called on legislators to enact voting rights legislation that would lead to the passing of the Voting Rights Act of 1965.

54. D: When certain groups of voters are put into as few districts as possible, this is considered to be a gerrymandering technique known as *packing*. This technique groups voters together to concentrate their voting strength and preference for a particular candidate or party in the packed district and to dilute or eliminate their voting power in other districts.

55. C: When district lines are created, each district should represent the population of the state, and each should have an equal number of people. This means that some districts might be large where the population is spread out, such as in rural areas, and small where the state is more densely populated, like in cities. If an even grid was created for the district lines, the districts would have very different populations with different demographics.

56. A: The word *partisan* means in favor of a particular political party or candidate. The passage states that most instances of gerrymandering are partisan and goes on to explain that racial gerrymandering is enacted to keep minorities from electing their preferred candidate. These lines would be drawn by the party in power to keep themselves in power.

57. B: To find the mean, or average, of the exchange rates, add all six numbers to get 5.338, then divide by 6:

$$0.923 + 0.848 + 0.893 + 0.877 + 0.846 + 0.951 = 5.338$$

$$5.338 \div 6 = 0.89$$

The median is the middle number once all the numbers have been put in order. With an even number of items in a data set, as in this case, the median is the average of the two middle numbers:

$$0.893 + 0.877 = 1.77$$

$$1.77 \div 2 = 0.885$$

The mean and median are very similar, so they are both good measures of central tendency. There are no repeated numbers in the data set, so there is no mode.

58. D: If the exchange rate of USD to EUR was lower in 2016 compared to 2017, one Euro could buy more US dollars, and the European Union would have been able to buy more goods from the US for the same amount of their currency in 2016 than in 2017. This would have likely resulted in the countries in the European Union buying more exports from the US that year.

59. D: President Obama referred to owing a debt to all who came before him and says that in no other country on Earth would his story be possible. He also mentioned his presence on the stage being "pretty unlikely." This is due to both his background and the steps that the US had made toward equality. Obama referred to pride based on the premise that "all men are created equal," and how this contributes to the greatness of the nation.

60. D: The US unemployment rate was not high in 1929, when it was less than 5%. However, it did increase rapidly in the years after 1929. It did not go up as much between 1932 and 1933 as it had in earlier years, but it did continue to go up, reaching 25% in 1933. The graph does not give any information about unemployment rates in other countries.